THE History
OF Media AND
Communication
Research

PETER LANG
New York • Washington, D.C./Baltimore • Bern
Frankfurt am Main • Berlin • Brussels • Vienna • Oxford

THE History OF Media AND Communication Research

CONTESTED MEMORIES

Edited by
David W. Park & Jefferson Pooley

PETER LANG
New York • Washington, D.C./Baltimore • Bern
Frankfurt am Main • Berlin • Brussels • Vienna • Oxford

Library of Congress Cataloging-in-Publication Data

The history of media and communication research: contested memories /
edited by David W. Park, Jefferson Pooley.
p. cm.
Includes bibliographical references and index.
1. Mass media—Research—History. 2. Communication—Research—History.
I. Park, David W. II. Pooley, Jefferson.
P91.3.H57   302.207'2—dc22   2007051150
ISBN 978-1-4331-0240-0 (hardcover)
ISBN 978-0-8204-8829-5 (paperback)

Bibliographic information published by **Die Deutsche Bibliothek**.
Die Deutsche Bibliothek lists this publication in the "Deutsche
Nationalbibliografie"; detailed bibliographic data is available
on the Internet at http://dnb.ddb.de/.

Cover design by Joshua Hanson

The paper in this book meets the guidelines for permanence and durability
of the Committee on Production Guidelines for Book Longevity
of the Council of Library Resources.

© 2008 Peter Lang Publishing, Inc., New York
29 Broadway, 18th floor, New York, NY 10006
www.peterlang.com

Printed in the United States of America

Dedication

To James W. Carey (1935–2006)

Acknowledgments

Edited volumes such as this are obviously the result of spread-out collaboration. Some of our collaborators do not, however, appear in the table of contents. For this reason, the editors wish to thank a number of others who made the volume possible.

Damon Zucca at Peter Lang was a source of inspiration and encouragement. When he left Peter Lang, he was replaced by Mary Savigar, whose patience and creativity made it enjoyable to work on the volume. Bernie Shade's assistance in all things technical was another essential element in putting this together. It would be hard to imagine a more supportive publishing team.

The volume springs indirectly from countless conversations with friends and academic co-conspirators, many of whom do not appear in this volume. The editors wish to thank, in particular, Fernando Bermejo, Jaap Bos, Mark Brewin, Craig Calhoun, Ray Fancher, Larry Gross, Meghan Grosse, Jen Horner, Steve Jones, Elihu Katz, Kurt and Gladys Lang, Carolyn Marvin, Neil McLaughlin, Jeff Olick, Petteri Pietikainen, Michael Schudson, and Eleanor Townsley. We are especially grateful to Sue Curry Jansen for her support and quiet wisdom.

The editors also recognize the special contribution of Peter Simonson, who introduced us to each other.

Finally, and most importantly, we thank our partners, Sarah Conner and Karen Beck Pooley. At the end of the day, they put up with us, whether or not we deserved it.

Dave Park & Jefferson Pooley

Table OF Contents

III. People and Places in the History of the Field

Foreword

HANNO HARDT

The field of communication studies has come of age, and with this new maturity comes the need to construct a genealogy of practices in a manner that explains and connects the various strands of fact and fiction, validates memory, and confirms intellectual identities to secure its place among the social sciences. The resulting "invention of tradition," to use Eric Hobsbawm's phrase,[1] is an institutional profile that not only reflects the accomplishments of the field but also identifies the disciplinary roots and their connections to what is now a considerable academic enterprise in the United States and elsewhere in the world.

Thus, communication studies has discovered history, not only as an essential instrument with which to forge the story of its own significance but also as a desirable form of authentication and legitimation in the intellectual community through a process of differentiation. After all, the perceived need for an identity involves the construction of a fiction that serves to place the institution—or the field of study—in reality. The published histories of communication studies authenticate and, together with the reproduction of compatible "key" texts as confirming evidence, help to reinforce the reigning explanation of the field's origins. Frequently, their tables of contents effectively illustrate the ideological range of the effort.

The essays in this book provide a welcome opportunity to reflect on how communication studies articulates its relationship to history, what contributes to the materialization of the past, and, more basically, what a history of communication studies is for. These questions are rarely, if ever, addressed, since communication studies arose out of a positivist paradigm of the social sciences during the early twentieth century with its prejudice against the value of a literary (or humanistic) discourse about communication in society. In the meantime, as Lyotard observes, living after the "grand récit," when the larger story of "the exigent unfolding of beginning, middle, and end no longer carries any currency" demands a new orientation in time and space, or, more specifically, a reconsideration of communication studies as historical narrative.[2]

Also, understanding the centrality of the historical account in the form of a history of communication studies becomes important at a time when skepticism about the value of historical knowledge—or anything else for that matter—feeds into a public uncertainty and generates recurring questions about whose history and in whose interest. And yet history is crucial, especially for a sense of identity among another generation of scholars in the field. Their search for an identity challenges the responsibility of a history of communication studies to produce relevant answers not only about its own role but also, for instance, about the place and time in which labels such as mass communication, communication, media studies, or cultural studies replaced older designations, such as journalism or speech. These were possibly administrative acts of differentiation to emphasize the distinctiveness of doing communication studies, but without much clarification regarding the nature of these developments.

History, according to Roland Barthes, is an ideological elaboration, and the received history of communication studies at this time only confirms the dominant belief that its presence is grounded in a continuity of practices associated with established and, therefore, credible representations of communication as a field of inquiry about the social, political, or cultural processes of society. Thus, the received history as a mode of understanding is an ideological construct, based on traditional views of doing history. The latter is a process of gathering facts and establishing a chronological order, which invites a classification of periods and the production of a narrative. This not only reflects the time and place of its beginning but is relative to the structure of communication studies.

The problems of doing a history of communication studies, however, are much older and grounded in the continuing debates regarding the nature of history, which has occupied modernist as much as postmodernist thought. Thus, it may be appropriate to note here that traditional views of writing history were confronted much earlier by American pragmatism and the New History of James Harvey Robinson in particular.[3] The latter considered the study of history a tool for change, providing opportunities for adaptation, or, as John Dewey suggests, "a lever for moving the present into a certain kind of future."[4] This perspective was modified by the rise of historical relativism, and the work of Charles Beard and Carl Becker, specifically, who questioned the belief in an objective rendition of the past and argued that the writing of history was an act of faith rather than a product of an objective social science.[5]

These developments are important reminders for a contemporary historiography of communication studies. They suggest the presence of a progressive approach to making history at a time when the idea of communication and the emerging conditions of a mass society became an interdisciplinary concern, which launched a research agenda pertaining to the role of media and communication in a democratic (American) society. Furthermore, it is also a reminder of the role of relativism, which has grown out of a lack of confidence in notions of truth or objectivity, and which resurfaces in the contemporary debates regarding the making of history.

The latter is frequently seen as a continuous process, reliant on the curiosity and insights of each generation, which seeks to describe the history of communication studies as a continuity. In fact, continuity as a guarantor of certainty has remained a characteristic of doing history, which is but a process of connecting with the past to explain the present conditions, if not the potential of the future. Consequently, communication studies becomes a historical narrative of successive, if not continuous, practices at the expense of contemplating the possibilities of discontinuity or, as Nietzsche suggests, acts of forgetting rather than remembering as a driving force in constructing history, in which perception is biased to deliver a calculated judgment. Michel Foucault calls it "effective" history, a history without constants, but with its focus on events in terms of their "most unique characteristics, their most acute manifestations."[6]

Indeed, what are the fictions of continuity in a history of communication studies? Which offer stability of the academic enterprise? And whose versions of the historical narratives prevail? These are guiding questions about its constructed history, which should inform the emerging idea of communication studies.

Thus, the past of communication studies emanates from various sources as a methodologically uniform and theoretically monolithic series of practices, despite its claims of interdisciplinarity. A dialog with individuals (biographies) and texts (documents and books or articles) produces an institutional history that is as much about establishing identity as about defining power. The result is a narrowly construed vision of communication studies, rooted in the traditional social sciences but with claims of liberation or independence, which have become manifest—despite Wilbur Schramm's initial skepticism—in the expressed idea of communication studies as a discipline. The latter, too, is an example of differentiation as a means of defining identity.

The more recent arrival of cultural studies (in the United States) and its reception, or rather co-optation, by communication studies has added a new dimension to the idea of change. It has done this by possibly expanding—if not redirecting—the very notion of communication studies as political, and considerations of ideology and power, in particular, as central to any understanding of communication as social practice.

In fact, the exclusionary tendency of a traditional history of communication studies, with its focus on leaders (e.g., "fathers") and on the explanatory nature of quantitative analyses of communication and media processes, associated its identity with the traditional social science apparatus that had dominated social inquiries during most of the twentieth century. Or, as Michel de Certeau (1988) reminds us, "history is entirely shaped by the place in which it is developed."[7] That place was occupied by entrenched interests in methodological conventions, borrowed from quantitative sociology, and distinguished by the paucity of theoretical debates. The latter are marked by a preoccupation with facts and chronological descriptions, reflecting the presence of technocratic ideals rather than creative impulses, which define the boundaries of historical explanation.

The return to culture, with the embrace of cultural studies and its larger ideological and political concerns, introduced a number of co-determinants of a new identity associated with a sense of engagement in social and political change. Their subsequent contributions to the potential materialization of a "new" history of communication studies can be found not only in the recognition of an anthropological or ethnographic dimension but also in literary and philosophical considerations of communication, all of which reinforce its centrality in human interaction.

In other words, the history of communication studies as a mode of understanding intellectual work on communication changes its site and draws on a large variety of interdisciplinary sources, among which Raymond Williams is as important as Wilbur Schramm or John Dewey, and Clifford Geertz, for instance, is as relevant as Ingmar Bergman and Cindy Sherman. Their work, standing in as examples for many others, reflects the intellectual and artistic efforts that have gone into the societal discourse about communication. They become part of the historical dimension of communication studies and give further credence to its fundamental role in exploring and interpreting society.

Thus, a critically relevant history of communication studies discloses the reversal of traditional prejudices and introduces the rise of a new identity from the interplay of disciplinary accounts regarding communication or, more generally, from the discontinuities of past narratives, or the quilt of cultural memory with its endless possibilities of explanation, its appreciation of fiction, and its roots in the politics of representation.

The arrival of postmodernism, which denies the grounding of (modernist or traditional) history in reality, reminds historians of communication studies of the relativity of their pursuit. But it also challenges their ideas of truth, or even contingent truths, and reveals the ideological dimension of historical work as concealed by methodology. Discrediting history as we know it allows for creating new histories in accordance with the interests and beliefs of their creators, who can draw on the political potential of postmodernism with its intrinsically antihumanistic stance. Under these conditions the history of communication studies as an orderly structure of discourse for the purpose of disseminating some truth about the past is reduced to a rhetorical product of the individual historian.

In either case, however, the history of communication studies as text fashions consciousness and may exert a considerable influence on defining identity. Thus, academic coursework, in particular, beyond any direct historiographical accounts of communication studies, with its choice of literature and its detailed interpretation of facts, which are laden with meaning, implicitly strengthens the dominant historical narrative. Teaching offers a suitable context for acquiring an intellectual identity, which is currently prone to be indistinguishable across the field of communication studies, since the latter by and large represents an ideologically homogeneous environment.

Exceptions are rare, but their presence allows for another kind of differentiation, one that shifts place and time for a distinctive perspective from which to consider the past and construct the present. Thus, the entry of Marxism into communication studies, however tentative, at the end of the twentieth century contained a new recognition of critique and historical scholarship vis-à-vis practical political goals. Here the received history of communication studies becomes a bourgeois narrative, endowed with the power of a discipline and its ideological fervor. A Marxist history of communication studies, on the other hand, embedded in an emancipatory project, insists on exposing the reigning theories and understandings that guide the dominant historical project and relies on pursuing issues of power within the historical reality of productive relations and types of social, economic, and political control. Such an approach, however, may well work against the (American) tendency to search for a common ground in which, as Alvin Gouldner put it, "historical development presumably occurs not through polemic, struggle, and conflict, but through consensus."[8]

These multiple realities for a contemporary history of communication studies, emerge from a general climate of skepticism and from the consequences of relativism in a pursuit of understanding one's intellectual identity in the academic community. They provide alternatives while addressing some familiar issues of doing history, and their presence suggests the potential for a constructive discourse regarding the form and function of a history of communication studies and the ways in which it could inform present practices.

More specifically, these reflections should also be a reminder of the noteworthy relationship between history and social theory. As disciplinary lines become blurred, communication theorists begin to draw on the analytical power of the historical narrative in their pursuit of understanding communication as a cultural phenomenon, citing Foucault, Bourdieu, Geertz, and Williams, among others, or turning to Marx and Weber, whose works contain a historical dimension.

Thus, doing history becomes a challenge and a responsibility for the historian of communication studies regardless of any particular ideological disposition. The challenge is to succeed in demystifying the function of the history of communication studies itself, for instance, while the responsibility lies in rendering interpretations that make a meaningful contribution to critically assessing the public role of communication studies. As James Carey suggested almost a generation ago, "the history of mass communication research is more than the history of 'findings' … [it] must include … a history of the changing world of mass communications: of the purposes to which these institutions are put, the audiences that gather to them, the social structures which they more or less shape."[9]

In other words, much remains to be done for a critical discourse about history that helps confront the social and political issues inherent in doing communication studies. In the meantime, it seems worth remembering that Walter Benjamin had it right when he insisted that the perspective from which we view the past will be shaped by the struggles in which we engage in the present.

NOTES

1. Hobsbawm and Terence, *The Invention of Tradition*.
2. Lyotard, *The Postmodern Condition*, 77.
3. See Robinson, *The New History*.
4. Dewey, *The Theory of Inquiry*, 238–239.
5. See Beard, "Written History as an Act of Faith"; Becker, *Every Man His Own Historian*.
6. Foucault, "Neitzche, Genealogy, History," 124.
7. Certeau, *The Writing of History*, 69.
8. Gouldner, *The Coming Crisis of Western Sociology*, 17.
9. Carey, "The Ambiguity of Policy Research," 441–442.

WORKS CITED

Beard, Charles. "Written History as an Act of Faith." *American Historical Review* 39 (1934): 219–229.

Becker, Carl. *Every Man His Own Historian: Essays on History and Politics*. New York: Crofts, 1935.

Carey, James W. "The Ambiguity of Policy Research: Social Research on Broadcasting." In *Communication Researchers and Policy-Making: An MIT Sourcebook*, edited by Sandra Braman, 437–444, Publication: 2003. Cambridge, MA: MIT Press.

Certeau, Michel de. *The Writing of History*. New York: Columbia University Press, 1988.

Dewey, John. *Logic: The Theory of Inquiry*. New York: Holt, 1938.

Foucault, Michel. "Nietzsche, Genealogy, History." In *The Postmodern History Reader*, edited by Keith Jenkins. London: Routledge, 1997.

Gouldner, Alvin. *The Coming Crisis of Western Sociology*. New York: Basic Books, 1970.

Hobsbawm, Eric and Ranger Terence (Eds.). *The Invention of Tradition.* Cambridge: Cambridge University Press, 1983.

Lyotard, Jean. *The Postmodern Condition: A Report on Knowledge.* Minneapolis: University of Minnesota Press, 1984.

Robinson, James Harvey. *The New History: Essays Illustrating the Modern Historical Outlook.* New York: Macmillan, 1912.

Introduction

JEFFERSON POOLEY AND DAVID W. PARK

"Strictly speaking, there is no history of mass communication research."

—JAMES W. CAREY[1]

Most of the published histories of mass communication studies are airbrushed and Whiggish. Accounts of the field's origins and development typically appear in textbook capsules and annual review essays, and tend to emphasize the progressive unfolding of a new science. Even the stirrings in the 1970s to challenge this progressivist narrative remained thoroughly presentist in other ways. Relative to the disciplinary history produced by the other social sciences, moreover, the historiography of mass communication research is anemic and notably unreflective. It is in this sense that James Carey's claim, quoted earlier, is true. Strictly speaking, there is very little history of mass communication research—at least the sort that takes the field's past as a serious object of study.

This volume is a response to Carey's lament about the field's neglect of its own past. The authors represented here, in the book's first section, "The State of the Historiography," address that neglect head-on. The volume's second and third sections ("Institutional Histories," "People and Places in the History of the Field") take up Carey's implicit challenge: these chapters exemplify a rigorous (if also catholic) approach to the history of the field. Taken together, the chapters collected here are meant to model, in a tentative way, the high standards that would characterize an emergent subdiscipline devoted to such study.

In this introduction, we briefly compare the history of communication research to the historical self-scrutiny of the other social sciences. We offer, in passing, some suggestions to help explain the field's relatively meager body of history. In the balance of the introduction, we propose a set of traits that a richer, more scholarly historiography might embody.

* * *

Complaints about the historiography of the social sciences form their own history. In 1965, George Stocking issued his well-known charter for a history less prone to "anachronism, distortion, misinterpretation, misleading analogy, neglect of context, oversimplication of process."[2] A year later, Robert Young published his fifty-page assault on the historiography of American psychology.[3] Robert K. Merton, a year after Young, reaffirmed his "history" versus "systematics" distinction in a classic essay that, among other things, urged historians of sociology to "extend beyond a chronologically ordered set of critical synopses of doctrine."[4] From the late 1960s on, a stream of critiques, of one or another discipline's published remembrances, has filled journals and edited volumes—in the form of origin-myth slayings,[5] survey-*cum*-critiques,[6] and, most systematically, a 1983 collection on *The Functions and Uses of Disciplinary History*.[7]

What's striking about this criticism is that it has, in a sense, been heeded. Stocking, Young, and Merton pointed to the sorry state of their respective disciplinary historiographies *forty years ago*. It is not surprising that the rigor, scope, and sophistication of historical work in each field—especially psychology, economics, and anthropology—has improved steadily in the decades since. In the past twenty-five years or so, all of the established social sciences have developed self-conscious subfields devoted to their histories. However marginal to their disciplines' centers, these subfields have nurtured, in every case, impressive work. In some disciplines, notably psychology and anthropology, researchers have erected a supporting infrastructure of associations, journals, archives, and specialized PhD programs.[8] The ideal of a community of critical peers engaged in a collaborative project—freqently invoked as a hollow bit of rhetoric—seems more or less realized in these other history of social science subfields. Professional historians, meanwhile, have helped to fill in some of the gaps between and across these established disciplines.[9]

Nothing like this exists for the history of communication research, despite the appearance, intermittently and in isolation, of fine scholarship.[10] The extant history of the field—most of it, anyway—is distinguished by unabashed engrossment with present concerns. Typically this means using history to establish scientific bona fides or the field's legitimate place in the university. For decades one staple of the field's self-narration, the claim that researchers at Columbia University during and after World War II replaced a mistaken faith in media omnipotence with measured findings of "limited effects," has for decades formed the core textbook contrast between naïve pre-history and the field's scientific coming-of-age.[11]

Deborah Lubken's contribution to this volume ("Remembering the Strawman") traces the active life of one of the stock epithets attached to that putative pre-history, the "hypodermic needle" theory of media influence. With a Mertonian eye for semantic nuance, Lubken shows how the label has been used—even by would-be revisionists—as a way to distinguish media researchers from the lay observer.

Wilbur Schramm, the mass communication field's major institution builder in the decades after the war, supplied another lasting narrative for a young, legitimacy-starved field.[12] Schramm's story was straightforward origin myth, complete with four eminent (and unwitting) "founders" said to have converged on a science of communication. Schramm's "four founders" myth is a near-perfect example of what Charles Camic has called strategic "predecessor selection,"[13] and this story, too, has enjoyed a long published afterlife. Lana Rakow's chapter ("Feminist Historiography and the Field") notes one of the consequences: these founders-by-ascription, all men, dominate the field's remembered past and blot out much else—including, notably, the history of feminist work and women researchers.

The history of mass communication research has been used, moreover, to grease the gears of paradigmatic succession—as a means, that is, to caricature, then batter, "old paradigm" whipping boys.[14] More often, the discipline's history is mined for usable genealogies, invoked by emergent approaches that present themselves as "recoveries." Here the work of James W. Carey in fashioning a "cultural approach" to communication on the shoulders, in part, of John Dewey, Charles Horton Cooley, and the Chicago School of sociology is an eloquent case in point.[15] Sue Curry Jansen's chapter "Walter Lippmann" establishes that we profoundly misremember Lippmann, and that this warped picture originates in a misleading historical trope, narrated by Carey and others, that pits an elitist Lippmann against Dewey the democrat.[16]

The point is that, for the field, the past has been an expedient—and a highly elastic one at that. The typical approach to writing history follows from this: a fast digest of a key idea or two, matched to thin and folksy biography. Core storylines are repeated, over and over, through uncited mnemonic hand-me-downs.[17] A bundle of canonic texts is often cited, but in a gestural, even totemic way, and archives, for the most part, remain undisturbed. Most of the existing history is so resolutely internalist that it ignores external *intellectual* influences, let alone social, political, and economic ones. In particular, the extremely interesting and revealing institutional history of the field has been neglected. The great bulk of the history, finally, has been written by active participants in the field, often central figures with their own legacies at stake.

Our complaint isn't that communication studies, alone, embellishes its past with helpful and heroic narratives in the service of teaching and legitimacy. All disciplines generate usable stories such as these.[18] It is all too easy, moreover, to admire the green grass of other social science subfields and to forget that these fields, in turn, may be coveting the verdant pastures of the history of science proper.[19] No, our complaint is that communication studies have the thin hagiography and *very little else*, whereas in the other social science fields the panegyrics are at least supplemented by bodies of good-faith historical research. In communication research, there is little alternative to, in Jennifer Platt's phrase, "the amateur history of unresearched introductory comments, taken-for-granted textbook versions and orally transmitted understandings."[20]

* * *

Why, then, has the historiography of communication research lagged behind its counterparts? One obvious factor is the field's relative youth as a self-conscious discipline—a status claimed (and attained in the most tentative way) only in the mid-1950s. The other social science disciplines are not much older, but they benefit from their emergence in tandem with the modern American university itself in the late nineteenth century. There is, because of these longer life-spans, simply more history to document, within disciplines that have had the chance, over the decades, to develop more refined divisions of scholarly labor. That fifty-year head start has also won these fields at least a partial exemption from the legitimacy crises that regularly beset communication research—so much so that the late nineteenth century seems shrouded, by comparison, in the misty recesses of time. These other disciplines, moreover, produced the same blend of origin myth and self-congratulation, in their own sometimes precarious early decades. The quality gap in disciplinary history may simply reflect a much broader pattern of delayed inheritance, whereby concepts and methods developed in established fields make their way, years later, to communication departments, with little reciprocity.[21]

There are additional, field-specific reasons for the robust historiographies in the other social sciences. Sociology, for example, has a distinct pedagogy of the classics, in which graduate training involves a one- or two-course encounter with the "holy trinity" (Marx, Durkheim, and Weber). This ongoing engagement, in which sociologists continue to wrestle with the likes of Weber, has supported genuinely historical attempts to contextualize these classics and their reception in the field. Psychology, though not nearly so substantively engaged with past luminaries, likewise requires a "history and systematics" course that has long supported a textbook and monographic market for history. For anthropology, a perpetual methodological crisis has generated a huge body of disciplinary self-reflection that has, predictably, involved historical self-scrutiny. Once formed, each discipline's history subfield then developed its own internal standards and organizational momentum.

Relative youth, and these field-specific factors, cannot do all the explanatory heavy lifting, however. Another, complementary explanation is suggested by John Durham Peters in his classic 1986 essay "The Institutional Sources of Intellectual Poverty in Communication Research." He argues by analogy to the nation-state and compares communication research to an "academic Taiwan"— claiming all of China from its own, much smaller island.[22] The field's sweeping and often hollow claims to a topic, "communication," are driven by the "urge to survive" and are built on institutional quicksand.[23] The paradox for Peters is that the field's desperate need for legitimacy precludes an honest coming-to-terms with its baleful organization. The result is self-perpetuating intellectual incoherence.

In that gloomy paper, Peters laments the "victory of institution over intellect in the formation of the field" and observes pointedly that communication research has omitted, in its disciplinary histories, the story of the field's tangled institutional emergence.[24] This history remains, at the time of writing, largely untold. If communication research has told one kind of story—the Whiggish—and left out most everything else, perhaps it is because the field has little otherwise, aside from the nebulous term itself, to hold it together.[25] Scattered across the university—and issued from a motley band of ancestors, of which speech and journalism are only the most prominent—communication has arguably needed what Edmund Burke called "pleasing illusions" more than the most other disciplines.[26] Tainted by vocational missions that, however, fill its lecture halls, programs in communication are both well off and in existential doubt. A single large university may have five or six distinct programs that carry the label, and a similar number of scholarly associations claim to represent the whole field.[27] A discipline assembled from (in Peters's words) "leftovers from earlier communication research married to dispossessed fields such as academic journalism, drama, or speech" needs memory more than it wants history.[28]

* * *

Is it fair to ask what a more serious and sensitive historiography would look like? In a list that is neither exhaustive nor additive, we propose a bundle of traits that good histories tend to express. Of course, no single work could, in check-list fashion, realize each of these properties. Many of the chapters collected in this volume do, however, exemplify one or more traits, as we suggest in the following text.

Qualified historicism. The best disciplinary histories attempt to reconstitute the ideas, figures, struggles over resources, and any other object of study, within the full context of their original location in space and time. This kind of good-faith effort is made, however, in the full knowledge that all such attempts will fall far short of the ideal, given the socially grounded limits of perspective, language, and narrative selection. All historical inquiry is motivated, at some level, by present concerns, and this is no cause for despair. As long as these motivations are tempered and, to the extent possible, explicitly acknowledged, they can be served without undue violence to the past.[29]

Wendy Worrall Redal's careful reconstruction ("Making Sense of Social Change") of British media research in the 1960s, within the context of the New Left's engagement with the postwar consumer culture, is an exemplar of this "qualified historicism" ideal. Redal acknowledges the limits of her study but draws on interviews, archival sources, and neglected secondary work to paint a far richer picture of post-war British media study than is provided by the Williams/Hoggart/Thompson great-books-exposition genre that stands in for the historiography of early British cultural studies.

Explanatory eclecticism. A narrowly conceived intellectual history approach is not, on its own, capable of explaining the trajectory of any given academic field. Nor, however, is the full complexity of a discipline exhausted with reference to strategic factors such as boundary work and credit seeking. Nonacademic audiences, government funders or commercial clients, the demands of students—all of these and many other factors besides give shape to disciplines and their intellectual products. However, these are empirical questions, more or less salient depending on the case. Good histories approach their topics as simultaneously social *and* cognitive in character and weigh one set of factors against another on the basis of evidence.

The chapters by Peter Simonson ("Writing Figures into the Field") and David Morrison ("Opportunity Structures and the Creation of Knowledge") provide a telling contrast. Simonson's chapter turns to the individual and his rhetoric as a device—one among many—to reconstruct aspects of the field's history. Simonson makes an eloquent and convincing historiographical case for this kind of approach and then illustrates its fecundity in a close reading of a neglected figure, Bill McPhee.

Morrison's chapter, in contrast, is cast in more sociological terms. "Why didn't Paul Lazarsfeld and the circle around him," Morrison asks, "conduct any real television research when the medium came on the scene in the 1950s?" He acknowledges that Lazarsfeld's intellectual disinterest played a role but tells a story of withdrawn funding in the climate of McCarthyism that, in this case at least, turned off a would-be research spigot.

Despite their rival approaches, Morrison's and Simonson's chapters share an openness to different kinds of evidence and explanation. This is crucial, if only because there is simply too much complexity and diversity within the modern academic arena, across fields and over time, for any unitary scheme to bear much explanatory burden.

Dirty fingernails. There is a great deal of untapped archival material, and as-yet unconducted oral history work, that should better inform histories of communication research. This means treating the existing narratives with skepticism—and as objects of study in and of themselves. Even attentive reading of well-known articles, scrutinized at the footnote level and with broader context in mind, can contribute to a rich and unconventional body of historical work.

J. Michael Sproule's contribution ("'Communication': From Concept to Field to Discipline") is a vivid case in point. Sproule's chapter refuses the customary trade-off between archival evidence and close reading, on the one hand, and substantive sweep and argumentative ambition, on the other. Similar to Sproule's well-known work on propaganda analysis, this chapter weaves documentary detail and nuance in with a larger narrative—in this case, a novel account of progressive disciplinary cohesion.

New, search-based methods. The published record of academic inquiry is fast becoming searchable in database form, and disciplinary historians are only just beginning to exploit this vast new trove of evidence. One obvious use is to trace key terms as they emerge and diffuse within and across fields; Deborah Lubken's qualitative history of the "hypodermic" metaphor, referenced earlier, clearly benefited from these new tools.

Long-established quantitative methods, such as citation analysis, are ripe for adaptation. James Anderson and Janet Colvin ("Media Research 1900–1945") build their chapter around a computer-assisted coding analysis of a large sample of the published media research of the early twentieth century. The study's ambitious scope is, in a sense, their reward: where traditional methods tend toward, at the limit, idiographic irrelevance, Anderson and Colvin are able to make qualified claims about decades-long trends.

Openness to institutional histories. Academic fields have a published face, but the daily life of department meetings, syllabus construction, appeals to the dean, and the like are often vital components of historical explanation. The focus need not be at the microlevel: broader patterns, such as field-specific reward systems, graduate program rivalries, or the role of vocational programs in land-grant universities, are crucial here too.

Veikko Pietilä, in his chapter ("How Does a Discipline Become Institutionalized?"), traces the distinct but related rise of research on mass communication in Germany and Finland. Central to Pietilä's densely sociological account is Richard Whitley's distinction between "cognitive" and "social" institutionalization.[30] Normally, Pietilä observes, a field forms around a bundle of topics and principles first, before assuming the trappings of an organized discipline. In the case of German newspaper science, however, the social institutionalization came first—so that the field had to cohere cognitively, after the fact. Pietilä's analysis here of the German and Finnish cases is, of course, richly suggestive for the American case.

More international and comparative histories. The published work in the history of media research is overwhelmingly concerned with the United States, Canada, and the rest of the Anglophone world. There is also a smaller literature on the Scandinavian, Dutch, German, and French cases. With an exception here and there, however, none of the extant histories attends to the field as it has developed in various non-Western countries. Nor is there any serious comparative work that places national traditions and institutional histories side by side.

Work that takes up these now-invisible national and regional histories will be valuable in itself. But the real rewards will come from the insights-by-contrast that comparative research generates. It would be fascinating, for example, to examine the influence of field organization on intellectual life (and vice versa)—to compare, for example, national traditions that have, as in the U.S. case, tethered their fields to professional schools, with those, such as the U.K. case, that have developed as standalone academic programs. Consider, too, the complex and uneven uptake of (and resistance to) Western research models and disciplinary histories in the post-colonial Third World university. Many other stories of international scope remain largely untold, including the involvement of communication researchers in various United Nations' forays into cultural policymaking. Kaarle Nordenstreng, in his contribution to the volume ("Institutional Networking"), brushes up against many of these research topics in his thorough history of the U.N.-linked scholarly association, the International Association for Media and Communication Research (IAMCR).

Dialogue with the historiography of the other social sciences. Communication research, wherever it has emerged in any stable, self-conscious form, has evolved first within the more established social sciences. In the twentieth-century U.S. case, psychology, sociology, and political science have housed in different ways and over sometimes distinct periods, housed major figures and approaches to media research. They have, moreover, supplied many of the personnel, research methods, and even strands of disciplinary memory that "communication," as a standalone field, adopted.

The silo-like isolation of historical work in each field has led the more established disciplines, in their chronicles, to neglect or distort media research. In a related way, research in the history of communication research tends to obscure the relevant disciplinary contexts and to project, instead, disciplinary self-consciousness onto periods—the 1930s, for example—when there was none. It is, to be sure, a tall order to tame the historical literature of a number of adjacent (and interpenetrating) fields, but the peculiar conditions of the field's evolution require it. For example, it would be impossible to reconstruct the context around Wilbur Schramm's frenetic institution building in the 1940s and 1950s without studying social scientists' wartime service, postwar confidence and scientism, and the interdisciplinary and foundation-linked network of elite scholars that gelled around cold war government service. In this context the story of communication research is, in some respects, the story of the social sciences more broadly.

One striking manifestation of the sealed-off historiographies is the Chicago School of sociology. The Chicago School's reflection and research on communication is largely missing from the otherwise methodical treatment by historians of sociology.[31] Browse the communication literature, however, and you get the impression that Chicago personalities such as Robert E. Park thought about nothing else. Here William Buxton's chapter ("From Park to Cressey") helps to bridge the gap between the two bodies of history. Buxton, who has published extensively in the history and sociology of both fields,[32] situates the school's communication thought in the context of interwar sociology. He concludes that the communication-related work of the Chicago "school" is far more diverse than the label suggests.

* * *

In putting this volume together, we invited John Durham Peters to reflect on his 1986 essay, and the result is a thoughtful, quasi-autobiographical chapter ("Institutional Opportunities for Intellectual History in Communication Studies"). Peters closes his chapter with a counterintuitive claim, that communication's status as a marginal latecomer may, in fact, open up intellectual space occluded by the confident myopia of more established disciplines. "Hegemony is epistemologically hazardous," he observes.

It is on this hopeful note that we introduce the volume. We reject the commonplace idea that the current progress of a field and its history are mutually destructive.[33] A more serious historiography of communication research would, it is true, be valuable for its own sake. The field's complex history is also, no doubt, a rich site for any historian curious about the twentieth-century American university or, say, the intersections of social science and cold war liberalism. Communication research—emerging as it did in response to a sequence of external pressures, from public concern, to government funding, to the industry's need for a workforce, to journalism schools' need for legitimacy, and so on—is also a kind of a sociology of knowledge exemplar and should interest those concerned with how the winners and losers in the scholarly knowledge game are chosen.

But it is the field itself, we contend, that has the most to gain from carefully conducted historical work. Neglected or long-buried veins of thought, for instance, might be tapped anew because of historical digging.[34] Lines of thought that have been transmitted in partial and misleading ways, likewise, might benefit from a more conscientious treatment.[35] Above all, honest scrutiny of our peculiar institutional roots will force a conversation about the intellectual consequences. The alternative, as Peters observed back in 1986, is head-in-the-sand irrelevance. This book is an attempt to start that long-overdue conversation.

NOTES

1. "The Chicago School and the History of Mass Communication Research," 14.
2. "On the Limits of 'Presentism' and 'Historicism,'" 215.
3. "Scholarship and the History of the Behavioural Sciences."
4. "On the History and Systematics of Sociological Theory," 34.
5. See, for example, George W. Stocking, "Matthew Arnold, E.B. Tylor, and the Uses of Invention"; Franz Samelson, "History, Origin Myth and Ideology"; Bruce Kuklick, "Myth and Symbol in American Studies"; and Kurt Danziger, "The Social Origins of Modern Psychology."
6. See Robert Alun Jones, "The New History of Sociology"; Mark Blaug, "On the Historiography of Economics"; and James Farr, "The History of Political Science."
7. Loren Graham et al.
8. Take the case of psychology: two journals (*History of Psychology* and *Journal of the History of the Behavioral Sciences*), a dedicated archival center at the University of Akron, two PhD programs (at the University of New Hampshire and York University), a History of Psychology division of the American Psychological Association, and a standalone scholarly association, Cheiron.
9. See, for example, Robert C. Bannister, *Sociology and Scientism*; Mark C. Smith, *Social Science in the Crucible*; Thomas L. Haskell, *The Emergence of Professional Social Science*; Dorothy Ross, *The Origins of American Social Science*; Theodore M. Porter and Dorothy Ross, *The Modern Social Sciences*.
10. There are a number of impressive works in the historiography of mass communication research, including the research of William Buxton, J. Michael Sproule, Timothy Glander, Brett Gary, and Rohan Samarajiva, discussed in Pooley's contribution to this volume ("The New History of Mass Communication Research"). Of the book-length and synoptic histories of the field, see Daniel Czitrom's *Media and the American Mind*; Willard Rowland's *The Politics of TV Violence*; Jesse Delia's "Communication Research: A History"; David Morrison's *The Search for a Method*; and Hanno Hardt's *Social Theories of the Press*. In the related area of public opinion research, Jean Converse's *Survey Research in the United States* remains indispensable, as is Sarah Igo's recent *The Averaged American*. Among other notable contributions are Kurt and Gladys Lang's work on European antecedents (e.g., "The European Roots"); John Durham Peters's sweeping intellectual history of the idea of communication (*Speaking into the Air*); Garth Jowett's work on the Payne Fund studies (e.g., "Social Science as a Weapon"); Peter Simonson's excavation of Robert K. Merton's communication thought (e.g., "The Serendipity of Merton's Communication Research") and his recently published *Annals* volume on *Personal Influence* ("Politics, Social Networks"); Karin Wahl-Jorgensen's work on communication study at the University of Chicago (e.g., "How Not to Found a Field"); and a number of under-appreciated dissertations (including Larry Jene King, "A History of the Department"; Barry Alan Marks, "The Idea of Propaganda"; David Morrison "Paul Lazarsfeld"; and Wendy Worrall Redal, "Imaginative Resistance"). A comprehensive online

bibliography of works in the history of communication research can be accessed at http://www.
historyofcommunicationresearch.org.

11. On this narrative, see Veikko Pietilä, "Perspectives on Our Past"; and Pooley, "Fifteen Pages that
Shook the Field."

12. Schramm first identified the "four founders" in a 1963 essay ("Communication Research in the
United States"), and he elaborated the account in many subsequent publications. Bernard Berelson
had named the four in his famous 1959 eulogy for the field ("The State of Communication
Research").

13. "Reputation and Predecessor Selection."

14. The classic example is Todd Gitlin's 1978 "Media Sociology: The Dominant Paradigm." See also
Pietilä, "Perspectives on Our Past," 350–52.

15. Carey lays out this narrative in a number of the essays collected as *Communication as Culture*, and
in some later work, including "The Chicago School."

16. Jansen's essay is longer than the others on account of its especially meticulous reconstruction of
Lippmann's thought. Jansen, in a related paper ("Phantom Conflict"), traces the spread of the
erstwhile "Lippmann–Dewey debate" in greater detail.

17. Everett Rogers's *A History of Communication Research*, for example, relies on "the general consensus of informed observers about who laid dominant roles in the history of communication
study." This is, as William Buxton has observed, "in effect, writing history backwards" ("Reaching
Human Minds," 177).

18. Robert Alun Jones: "Sociology, like all emergent scientific disciplines, has generated a largely
mythological past which performs the important functions of legitimating present practice and
reinforcing the solidarity of its practitioners" ("On Merton's 'History' and 'Systematics,'" 121);
and Ulfried Geuter: "the implicit and common approach to the history of psychology is to com-
memorate its progenitors and to institute a tradition of 'great men' and their 'great ideas,' an
important factor of the disciplinary ego" ("The Uses of History," 193–94).

19. Here is Alan Sica, commenting on the historiography of sociology: "There are no definitive,
comprehensive histories of sociology as practiced in the United States (or elsewhere) which can be
compared favorably with the leading extant accounts of biology, chemistry, economics, philosophy,
or psychology" ("Defining Disciplinary Identity," 713).

20. *A History of Sociological Research Methods*, 33.

21. Willard Rowland observed such a lag many years ago: "In many instances developments in communication research have lagged a decade or so behind the 'parent' sciences, but even in those
cases in which the association has been closer in time, the trend has been one of imitation and
following" (*The Politics of TV Violence*, 21–22).

22. 543.

23. Ibid., 538.

24. Ibid.

25. This argument is elaborated in Pooley's chapter ("The New History of Mass Communication
Research") in this volume.

26. *Reflections on the Revolution in France*, 67.

27. One consequence of this is that the labels meant to designate our ostensible object of study—
"communication," "communication research," "communication studies," "mass communication
research," and so on—are slippery and in important respects partial. Each refers to many things
and, arguably, nothing at all. It is true that this nomenclatural disarray begs for historical work on
the terms' evolutions. For this volume, we are resigned to cycle through labels—a "communication

research" here, a "mass communication study" there—in full knowledge that the labels' referents are shifting and often murky.

28. "Institutional Sources," 543. James Anderson has made a complementary point: "The disarray of our history would seem to be quite representative of our present state. In fact, I would argue that it is our present state that forces the disorganization of our history" ("The Caravan of Communication," 282).

29. The stance evoked here resonates with George Stocking's notion of "enlightened presentism" and is compatible, too, with a view of history writing grounded in the hermeneutics of Hans-Georg Gadamer, in which a scholar forms a "fusion of horizons" with his object of study (see *Truth and Method*; Charles Taylor, "Gadamer on the Human Sciences"; and Martin Jay, "Should Intellectual History Take a Linguistic Turn?").

30. "Cognitive and Social Institutionalization."

31. See, for example, Martin Bulmer's *The Chicago School of Sociology*, as well as Andrew Abbott's brilliant history of the historiography of the Chicago School, in *Department and Discipline*, 4–33.

32. Including an important treatment of Talcott Parsons, *Talcott Parsons and the Capitalist Nation-State*.

33. Recall Robert Merton's epigraph for *Social Theory and Social Structure*: "'A science which hesitates to forget its founders is lost,' Alfred N. Whitehead" (1).

34. As Wolf Lepenies and Peter Weingart observe, "One form of reaction and, sometimes, consolation consists in the re-historization of a field. In retrospect, hitherto neglected and hidden alternatives to the mainstream of scientific development become visible and attempts are made to re-interpret the cognitive identity of a discipline or even to re-invent it as a whole as has been the case with anthropology" (Introduction, xiii).

35. Stocking, in 1965, made this point: "By suspending judgment as to present utility, we make the judgment ultimately possible" ("On the Limits," 217).

WORKS CITED

Abbott, Andrew D. *Department & Discipline: Chicago Sociology at One Hundred*. Chicago: University of Chicago Press, 1999.

Anderson, James A., Douglas Birkhead, David L. Eason, and Mary S. Strine. "The Caravan of Communication and Its Multiple Histories." In *Advancing Communication Science: Merging Mass and Interpersonal Processes*, edited by Robert Hawkins, John M. Wiemann, and Suzanne Pingree, 267–307. Newbury Park, CA: Sage, 1988.

Bannister, Robert C. *Sociology and Scientism: The American Quest for Objectivity, 1880–1940*. Chapel Hill: University of North Carolina Press, 1987.

Berelson, Bernard. "The State of Communication Research." *Public Opinion Quarterly* 23, no. 1 (1959): 1–5.

Blaug, Mark. "On the Historiography of Economics." *Journal of the History of Economic Thought* 12 (1990): 27–37.

Bulmer, Martin. *The Chicago School of Sociology: Institutionalization, Diversity, and the Rise of Sociological Research*. Chicago: University of Chicago Press, 1984.

Burke, Edmund. *Reflections on the Revolution in France*. Indianapolis, IN: Hackett, 1987.

Buxton, William J. *Talcott Parsons and the Capitalist Nation-State: Political Sociology as a Strategic Vocation*. Toronto: University of Toronto Press, 1985.

————. "Reaching Human Minds: Rockefeller Philanthropy and Communications, 1935–1939." In *The Development of the Social Sciences in the United States and Canada: The Role of Philanthropy*, edited by Theresa R. Richardson and Donald Fisher, 177–92. Stamford, CT: Ablex, 1999.

Camic, Charles. "Reputation and Predecessor Selection: Parsons and the Institutionalists." *American Sociological Review* 57, no. 4 (1992): 421–45.

Carey, James W. *Communication as Culture: Essays on Media and Society*. Boston: Unwin Hyman, 1989.

————. "The Chicago School and the History of Mass Communication Research." In *James Carey: A Critical Reader*, edited by Eve Stryker Munson and Catherine A. Warren, 14–33. Minneapolis: University of Minnesota Press, 1997.

Converse, Jean M. *Survey Research in the United States: Roots and Emergence 1890–1960*. Berkeley: University of California Press, 1987.

Czitrom, Daniel J. *Media and the American Mind: From Morse to McLuhan*. Chapel Hill: University of North Carolina Press, 1982.

Danziger, Kurt. "The Social Origins of Modern Psychology." In *Psychology in Social Context*, edited by Allan R. Buss, 27–45. New York: Irvington, 1979.

Delia, Jesse G. "Communication Research: A History." In *Handbook of Communication Science*, edited by C. R. Berger and S. H. Chaffee, 20–98. Newbury Park, CA: Sage, 1987.

Farr, James. "The History of Political Science." *American Journal of Political Science* 32 (1988): 1175–195.

Gadamer, Hans-Georg. *Truth and Method*. London: Sheed & Ward, 2002.

Geuter, Ulfried. "The Uses of History for the Shaping of a Field: Observations on German Psychology." In *Functions and Uses of Disciplinary Histories*, edited by Loren Graham, Wolf Lepenies, and Peter Weingart, 191–228. Boston: D. Reidel, 1983.

Gitlin, Todd. "Media Sociology: The Dominant Paradigm." *Theory and Society* 6 (1978): 205–53.

Graham, Loren R., Wolf Lepenies, and Peter Weingart eds. *Functions and Uses of Disciplinary Histories*. Boston: D. Reidel and Kluwer, 1983.

Hardt, Hanno. *Social Theories of the Press: Constituents of Communication Research, 1840s to 1920s*. 2nd ed. Lanham, MD: Rowman & Littlefield, 2001.

Haskell, Thomas L. *The Emergence of Professional Social Science: The American Social Science Association and the Nineteenth-Century Crisis of Authority*. Urbana: University of Illinois Press, 1977.

Igo, Sarah E. *The Averaged American: Surveys, Citizens, and the Making of a Mass Public*. Cambridge, MA: Harvard University Press, 2007.

Jansen, Sue Curry. "Phantom Conflict: Lippmann, Dewey and the Fate of the Public in Modern Society." Unpublished paper, Muhlenberg College, 2007.

Jay, Martin. "Should Intellectual History Take a Linguistic Turn? Reflections on the Habermas-Gadamer Debate." In *Modern European Intellectual History: Reappraisals and New Perspectives*, edited by Dominick LaCapra and Steven L. Kaplan, 86–110. Ithaca, NY: Cornell University Press, 1982.

Jones, Robert Alun. "On Merton's 'History' and 'Systematics' of Sociological Theory." In *Functions and Uses of Disciplinary Histories*, edited by Loren Graham, Wolf Lepenies, and Peter Weingart, 121–42. Boston: D. Reidel, 1983.

————. "The New History of Sociology." *Annual Review of Sociology* 9 (1983): 447–69.

Jowett, Garth. "Social Science as a Weapon: The Origins of the Payne Fund Studies, 1926–1929." *Communication* 13 (1992): 211–25.

King, Larry Jene. "A History of the Department of Communication at the University of Oklahoma: A Case Study in the History of the Discipline." PhD diss., University of Oklahoma, 1990.

Kuklick, Bruce. "Myth and Symbol in American Studies." *American Quarterly* 24, no. 4 (1972): 435–50.

Lang, Kurt. "The European Roots." In *American Communication Research*, edited by Everette E. Dennis and Ellen Wartella, 21-38. Mahwah, NJ: Lawrence Erlbaum, 1996.

Lepenies, Wolf, and Peter Weingart. Introduction to *Functions and Uses of Disciplinary Histories*, edited by Loren Graham, Wolf Lepenies, and Peter Weingart, ix–xx. Boston: D. Reidel, 1983.

Marks, Barry Alan. "The Idea of Propaganda in America." PhD diss., University of Minnesota, 1957.

Merton, Robert K. "On the History and Systematics of Sociological Theory." In *On Theoretical Sociology: Five Essays, Old and New*, 1–37. New York: Free Press, 1967.

———. *Social Theory and Social Structure*. Enlarged ed. New York: Free Press, 1968.

Morrison, David. "Paul Lazarsfeld: The Biography of an Institutional Innovator." PhD diss., University of Leicester, 1976.

———. *The Search for a Method: Focus Groups and the Development of Mass Communication Research*. Luton, UK: University of Luton Press, 1998.

Peters, John Durham. "Institutional Sources of Intellectual Poverty in Communication Research." *Communication Research* 13, no. 4 (1986): 527–59.

———. *Speaking into the Air: A History of the Idea of Communication*. Chicago: University of Chicago Press, 1999.

Pietilä, Veikko. "Perspectives on Our Past: Charting the Histories of Mass Communication Studies." *Critical Studies in Mass Communication* 11 (1994): 346–61.

Platt, Jennifer. *A History of Sociological Research Methods in America: 1920–1960*. Cambridge: Cambridge University Press, 1996.

Porter, Theodore M., and Dorothy Ross, eds. *The Modern Social Sciences*. Cambridge: Cambridge University Press, 2003.

Redal, Wendy Worrall. "Imaginative Resistance: The Rise of Cultural Studies as Political Practice in Britain." PhD diss., University of Colorado at Boulder, 1997.

Rogers, Everett M. *A History of Communication Study: A Biographical Approach*. New York: Free Press, 1994.

Ross, Dorothy. *The Origins of American Social Science*. Cambridge: Cambridge University Press, 1991.

Rowland, Willard D., Jr. *The Politics of TV Violence: Policy Uses of Communication Research*. Beverly Hills, CA: Sage, 1983.

Samelson, Franz. "History, Origin Myth and Ideology: 'Discovery' of Social Psychology." *Journal for the Theory of Social Behavior* 4, no. 2 (1974): 217–32.

Schramm, Wilbur. "Communication Research in the United States." In *The Science of Human Communication*, edited by Wilbur Schramm, 1–16. New York: Basic Books, 1963.

Sica, Alan. "Defining Disciplinary Identity: The Historiography of U.S. Sociology." In *Sociology in America: A History*, edited by Craig Calhoun, 713–31. Chicago: University of Chicago Press, 2007.

Simonson, Peter. "The Serendipity of Merton's Communication Research." *International Journal of Public Opinion Research* 17, no. 3 (2005): 277–97.

———, ed. "Politics, Social Networks, and the History of Mass Communications Research: Rereading *Personal Influence*," special issue. *Annals of the American Academy of Political and Social Science* 608 (2006).

Smith, Mark C. *Social Science in the Crucible: The American Debate over Objectivity and Purpose, 1918–1941*. Durham, NC: Duke University Press, 1994.

Stocking, George W. "Matthew Arnold, E.B. Tylor, and the Uses of Invention." *American Anthropologist* 65 (1963): 783–99.

————. "On the Limits of 'Presentism' and 'Historicism' in the Historiography of the Behavioral Sciences." *Journal of the History of the Behavioral Sciences* 1 (1965): 211–17.

Taylor, Charles. "Gadamer on the Human Sciences." In *The Cambridge Companion to Gadamer*, edited by Robert J. Dostal, 126–42. Cambridge: Cambridge University Press, 2002.

Wahl-Jorgensen, Karin. "How Not to Found a Field: New Evidence on the Origins of Mass Communication Research." *Journal of Communication* 54 (2004): 547–64.

Whitley, Richard. "Cognitive and Social Institutionalization of Scientific Specialties and Research Areas." In *Social Processes of Scientific Development*, edited by Richard Whitley, 69–95. London: Routledge & Kegan Paul, 1974.

Young, Robert M. "Scholarship and the History of the Behavioural Sciences." *History of Science* 2 (1966): 1–51.

I. STATE OF THE HISTORIOGRAPHY

CHAPTER ONE

Remembering THE Straw Man: The Travels AND Adventures OF *Hypodermic*[1]

DEBORAH LUBKEN

I cannot refrain from repeated reminders that this frequently cited theory never really had any followers among persons we would consider social scientists. But it was congruent with the popular fears about the effectiveness of the propaganda of totalitarian regimes and was used as a straw man that helped dramatize conclusions drawn from empirical findings in a U.S. context and make them appear more novel than they actually were. The theory has been buried rhetorically a countless number of times.

—KURT LANG

Straw men are perplexing creatures. Substantively flimsy and structurally unsophisticated, their histories are literally inscribed for them in conditions not of their own choosing. Yet straw men are uncommonly resistant to rhetorical burying. As progeny of discourse, they flourish in the very arguments asserting their demise.

Such is the case with the theory of "the supposedly 'all-powerful' media" to which Kurt Lang refers.[2] Identified by a number of labels, *hypodermic* and *bullet* the two most popular, the model has been—and continues to be—subjected to a battery of symbolic thrashing by communication researchers, invariably emerging no worse for wear. Exposing the model's "straw man" status, a project to which some of the biggest names in the field have contributed, has also proven largely ineffective. In addition to Lang, Steven H. Chaffee and John L. Hochheimer call the "'hypodermic needle' and 'magic bullet' images" into question, contending that both labels "represent misinterpretations of metaphors drawn from medicine, and appear to have been 'straw men' created some years later as a naïve conception against which the limited-effects model could be contrasted."[3] Similarly, George Gerbner argues that these metaphors "were set up as straw men with which to deride the concern about media power" in the aftermath of World War II.[4] Yet the "straw man" remains conspicuously unburied. The model's presence in the field's literature is pervasive: as a standard plot device in narratives about the past, as a bold-faced term elaborated in the glossary sections of textbooks, and as an all-purpose invective in book reviews.

This persistence can be explained, in part, by the model's place in the field's history telling, where it is used to define and maintain present-day divisions between research paradigms. Jeffrey L. Bineham takes this position, arguing that how scholars think about the hypodermic model influences how they understand the field's evolution and, consequently, their own theoretical and methodological choices. Researchers who view the model as a straw man typically identify with the empirical effects camp, observes Bineham, while those who accept the "received version" of the field's history tend toward the critical tradition.[5] This explanation is tenable, particularly for certain debates over the model's origins, but it does not sufficiently account for the prevalent invocation of needles and bullets in other contexts.

In much of the field's literature, the bullet and hypodermic needle metaphors are treated in tandem (and often interchangeably) with each other and with a handful of other analogies. My own approach to the enigma of the "straw man's" longevity requires discriminating between the needles, bullets, conveyor belts, and "click-click; push-pull" mechanisms.[6] Since, by my accounting, *hypodermic* has enjoyed the longest use, the remaining labels are left to future inquiry. I begin from the premise that the hypodermic model—whether an accurate representation of early researchers' thinking or a foil erected by the "limited effects" tradition—is constituted in discourse. It follows that the place to begin searching for answers to questions about the hypodermic model is not in some interwar soup stocked with propaganda analysis and assorted European theories; the place to begin is the point in the field's literature at which media effects were first described in terms of a hypodermic injection.

At first blush, identifying the earliest description of media effects in these terms should be a relatively simple endeavor, given the narrowly circumscribed domain of inquiry. The hypodermic needle (as a medical instrument) was not invented until the 1850s and did not enjoy widespread use in the United States until the 1860s,[7] mass communication research is less than a century old, and discussion of the field's history has even more recent beginnings. But the matter is more complicated than it initially seems, and answers have been obscured over time by habits and practices endemic to reading and writing history. As is often the case in such situations, the process of untangling an ostensibly simple problem led to more interesting questions: When did the *metaphor* of injected message content calcify into a *label*, emancipated from explicit metaphorical entailments? When did this type of media effect acquire its inordinate power? How did the earliest references to injections and hypodermic stimuli fade from the field's memory, and how did other writings assume notoriety as source of the label *hypodermic?*

In consulting and, consequently, comparing the references necessary to pursue the above inquiries, I began to question the uniformity of the model behind the label—the existence of a shared signified to which the *hypodermic* sign is applied—and commenced upon a Merton-esque squirreling away of references for subsequent analysis.[8] After examining hypodermic effects in more than 120 sources to assess characteristics of audiences, features of media influence, and the identities of those purported to have believed in hypodermic effects, I concluded that the model's resilience is not so perplexing. The "straw man's" multiple backstories, shifty profile, and imperviousness to the efforts of rhetorical grave-diggers are testaments to the model's active use by contemporary communication researchers to maintain the boundaries of the scholarly field, although I map this boundary maintenance differently than does Bineham. Ultimately, I contend that the "straw man" (the hypodermic model) and exposés of the "straw man" serve the same purpose: to defend against incursions from other academics who study media and from the specter of the general public.

THE EARLY YEARS: FROM "SUBTLE POISON" TO THE "GIANT HYPODERMIC NEEDLE"

Even if a body of writing constituting the "mass communication research literature" could be precisely demarcated and agreed upon, searching every text for a hypodermic needle analogy borders on the impossible. For the time being, I am limited to proffering likely first references and debunking spurious points of origin, although the increasing availability and indexing of electronic texts may facilitate future searches for the introduction of this and other metaphors to the field's literature.

In academic publications, the earliest allusions to media influence as an injection emphasize the power of the *communicator*—in both examples below, a U.S. president—over that of the *media* through which message content is disseminated.[9] Harold Lasswell, in his 1927 study of World War I propaganda, writes that Woodrow Wilson ("the great generalissimo on the propaganda front") "brewed the subtle poison which industrious men injected into the veins of a staggering [German] people, until the smashing powers of the Allied armies knocked them into submission."[10] The role of media is likewise unspecified by Philip E. Jacob in a 1940 article on the relationship between world events (primarily incidents of Axis aggression and U.S. responses) and Americans' views toward neutrality:

> In opening the special session of Congress on September 21, the President had made one of his most forceful appeals to end the arms embargo. Roosevelt's effect upon public opinion was not permanent, however, but acted like a temporary hypodermic.[11]

When compared with the accent on powerful, direct effects so common in later hypodermic lore, these early references by Lasswell and Jacob cast the media as relatively impotent. In the case of Lasswell's comments, the "poison" of propaganda was "subtle"—a stopgap means of holding off an already weakened German population until full Allied military intervention. The impact of President Roosevelt's appeal, cited by Jacob, is likewise fleeting.

References to more powerful hypodermic effects made their way into education journals a year later, after a *Chicago Daily News* op-ed piece by Sterling North on the "poisonous mushroom growth" in comic reading by children spurred debate among education researchers. In the editorial, which first ran on May 8, 1940, North rails against comics for stealing money from children's pockets, straining young eyes and nervous systems, and spoiling children's natural sense of color. Underlying these charges is an implied link between comic reading and violence. Comic magazines' "hypodermic injection of sex and murder make [*sic*] the child impatient with better, though quieter stories," warns North. To avoid raising "a coming generation even more ferocious than the present one," parents and teachers must intervene with the "antidote" of classic, quality literature.[12] The academic responses to the issues raised by North vary, but at least three contributors to education journals directly quote his remark about "hypodermic injections of sex and murder," although none repeats the metaphor in their own words.[13]

The earliest use of *hypodermic* by a mass communication researcher to describe powerful media influence on a vulnerable audience appears to be in a 1953 report of Columbia's Bureau of Applied Social Research (BASR) written by Elihu Katz, then a graduate student, for the Implementation Committee on Television.

> Exaggerating only slightly, we might say that the "model" of the campaign-like persuasion process which research had in mind, at least at the outset, resembled nothing so much as it resembled a giant hypodermic needle. Until very recently, it was widely assumed that the media were all-powerful, capable of reaching out, and influencing nearly every eye and ear.

Katz elaborates the model's composition in subsequent pages, summarizing as follows:

> In short the model of the mass persuasion process looked like this: There were the powerful mass media, on one hand, sending forth their message, and the atomized mass of individuals, on the other, rather directly and immediately responding—and nothing in between.[14]

Katz's 1953 report is clearly an early version of the first part of *Personal Influence*, the media research classic he coauthored with Paul Lazarsfeld, but the hypodermic needle reference was dropped before *Personal Influence* was published in 1955.[15] Although Katz's report was not widely distributed, a reference to a hypodermic injection did make its way into the pages of another, highly cited BASR publication: *Voting*, the Bureau's analysis of the 1948 presidential campaign, published in 1954.[16] In the introductory paragraphs of a chapter on political processes, the authors comment that "typical debates about the role of the media too often imply a simple, direct 'influence'—like a hypodermic stimulus on an inert subject—and that is a naïve formulation of the political effects of mass communications."[17]

Similar to Katz's "it resembled a giant hypodermic needle," *Voting*'s "like a hypodermic stimulus on an inert subject" employs the full efficacy of metaphorical comparison, issuing an invitation to understand one thing (the political effects of mass communications) in terms of another (a hypodermic injection). With subsequent use, however, the metaphor calcified into a label, with the adjective *hypodermic* as its primary component. As early as 1957, the Bureau's Joseph T. Klapper announced that the orientation of mass communication research was shifting away from "the concept of 'hypodermic effect,'"[18] and by the early 1960s, the term was regularly flanked by quotation marks but unaccompanied by a citation. David K. Berlo's treatment is typical of how the label came to appear in the field's literature: "Much of the early discussion of the effects of the mass media of communication were [*sic*] of the 'hypodermic-needle' variety."[19]

Untethered from a specific source, *hypodermic* ranged freely in the pages of the field's journals and books and began to take up residence in the "H" sections of indexes and glossaries. A generation later, perhaps motivated by an impulse to chronicle more precisely the field's past, retrospective accounts of the label's coinage began to surface. The emergence and diffusion of these narratives is addressed in the following section.

NEW LEASES ON LIFE: THE PART PLAYED BY PROSE

Apart from the scale of the field's literature, the primary obstacle to locating the first use of *hypodermic* is the difficulty of distinguishing between references to the label itself and references to the model of media influence to which the label is commonly applied. Disentangling a metaphor from the object to which it lends meaning can be tricky, particularly when the two have been paired for decades. In the case of *hypodermic*, several factors further complicate this process.

As mentioned previously, *hypodermic* is used interchangeably with a number of other labels, most often variants of *bullet*.[20] At a commonsense level, bullets differ considerably from needles. One might observe, for example, that the former resembles a message while the latter can be taken for a medium. Nevertheless, the two labels are commonly cross-referenced in indexes and glossaries, and in standard prose it is not unusual for needles and bullets to intermingle with considerable freedom, as in the following textbook explanation of the "magic bullet theory" in terms of hypodermic injections:

> The magic bullet theory, sometimes called the hypodermic needle theory, alleged that ideas from the media were in direct causal relation to behavior. The theory held that the media could inject ideas into someone the way liquids are injected through a needle.[21]

The transposability of bullets and needles is symptomatic of a larger tendency to equate both labels with the model of media influence they are used to describe. *Bullet* can stand in for powerful and direct effects on a passive audience, which can, in turn, be substituted for *hypodermic*. In the aftermath of such exchanges, it can be difficult to distinguish label from model.

Differentiating between label and model is further complicated by writing conventions—notably the use of quotation marks—and by common (although not ideal) reading habits. More often than not, *hypodermic* is framed in quotation marks, which can be used to offset words or phrases for a number of reasons. The most common usage in academic writing is to identify material that is directly quoted from another source, but an alternate purpose is to call attention to words or phrases that the author is using in an unconventional way, such as coined expressions or key terms. Context is often the only clue for indicating which way a particular set of quotation marks should be interpreted. In the case of references to the hypodermic model, a cursory reading is frequently not adequate to determine which use of quotation marks is intended, as illustrated in the following excerpt from a popular edited volume on media effects:

> Mass communications historians tell us that the earliest models of communication effects posited that communications were very powerful: the early "bullet" or "hypodermic needle" models of mass communication (Katz & Lazarsfeld, 1955, p. 16) that gave rise to the earliest conception of communication effects: who says what to whom through what medium with what effects.[22]

Since Katz and Lazarsfeld use neither *bullet* nor *hypodermic needle* on page 16 of *Personal Influence*, the quotation marks are clearly being used to signal nonstandard use, but without reading the original text it is easy to assume that Katz and Lazarsfeld employed—and even coined—both labels.

Identifying the coinage of the label is complicated by a final factor unrelated to the label-model distinction: the particular type of history-telling inhabited by *hypodermic*. The shortcomings of the field's historiography are addressed at some length elsewhere in the present volume, so here I comment only that accounts of the hypodermic model tend to serve as familiar, obligatory pit stops in sparsely referenced narratives en route to other topics and arguments. As a result, writing in which the label appears is perhaps more prone to minutial inaccuracies, such as incorrect page numbers in citations, than the larger body of mass communication literature.

During my search for the origin of *hypodermic*, two books, Katz and Lazarsfeld's *Personal Influence* and Lasswell's *Propaganda Technique in the World War* (hereafter *Propaganda*), were repeatedly suggested in both print and conversation as texts in which the label was coined. Although *hypodermic* appears in neither book, their (mis)identification as the source of the label can be explained, at least in part, by the factors elaborated above.

* * *

There is little doubt that the first chapter of *Personal Influence* has contributed, perhaps more than any other work, to the history of mass communication research in general and, more specifically, to the field's conceptualization of the hypodermic model. These "Fifteen Pages That Shook the Field" are widely acknowledged as the seminal installment of the field's received history and, according to Jefferson Pooley, have had "more influence on the field's historical self-understanding than anything published before or since."[23] What is puzzling is how these influential fifteen pages came to be known as the source of *hypodermic*. As discussed in the previous section, the idea of powerful mass media exerting direct influence over a vulnerable, atomized audience transferred neatly from Katz's 1953 BASR report to the text of *Personal Influence*, but the "giant hypodermic needle" did not survive the editing process. How and when did *hypodermic* seep into the collective memory of those influential fifteen pages?

The "when" of the above question is easy enough to answer—the retrospective link between the hypodermic model and *Personal Influence* seems to have formed during the early to mid-1960s—but the "how" is more difficult to specify. Late 1950s and early 1960s references to the label do not link it to *Personal Influence*. Klapper references *Voting* when he cites "hypodermic effects" in both *The Effects of Mass Communication* and an earlier journal article.[24] Berlo writes about "'hypodermic needle' concepts of how communication works," but cites no one, and his language does not evoke the *Personal Influence* account.[25] Likewise, contemporaneous sources that cite Katz and Lazarsfeld's account of power-ful effects do not use *hypodermic*. Raymond A. and Alice H. Bauer, for example, quote *Personal Influence* at length in laying out their own account of the "myth of the omnipotent media," but at no point do they mention needles or injections.[26]

By the mid-1960s, however, *hypodermic* and *Personal Influence* begin to appear together. In 1966, for example, Melvin L. DeFleur's *Theories of Mass Communication* lists "hypodermic needle theory" alongside "transmission belt the-ory" and criticizes Katz and Lazarsfeld for oversimplifying the model with such labels, an indication that the link between *hypodermic* and *Personal Influence* was already in place at the time of DeFleur's writing.[27]

Over time, the hypodermic model and *Personal Influence* have become closely associated. As a result, the book is often presented not just as a source for the model but also as the text in which the label was coined. Anecdotal evidence col-lected during my search suggests that, particularly for communication scholars beginning their careers in the late 1970s and after, the connection was forged between *hypodermic* and *Personal Influence* when Todd Gitlin squared off with the "dominant paradigm" in his notorious 1978 broadside. Gitlin's essay is relevant in multiple pedagogical contexts—and therefore excellent syllabi fodder for theory, research methods, cultural studies, and history courses—in which it is not always read alongside its object of criticism. In fact, Peter Simonson has remarked that it is not uncommon for communication scholars, particularly those in the cultural studies tradition, to first learn of *Personal Influence* through Gitlin's critique.[28]

When read alongside *Personal Influence*, Gitlin's essay is an illuminating exam-ple of how quotation mark–generated ambiguity—in conjunction with less-than-assiduous reading habits—has contributed to spurious accounts of *hypodermic*'s coinage. Gitlin turns his attention to the hypodermic model immediately follow-ing an opening sally against "limited effects" research, under the heading, "The 'Hypodermic' Theory." The excerpt below appears exactly as printed in Gitlin's article, with Gitlin's endnotes bracketed to distinguish them from the footnotes of the present chapter.

> The "personal influence" paradigm is itself located within a critique of the ear-lier "hypodermic" theory, which is in turn both a theory of society and a theory of the workings of mass media within it.[14] In the "hypodermic" model, society is mass society, and mass communications "inject" ideas, attitudes, and dispositions towards behavior into passive, atomized, extremely vulnerable individuals. Katz and Lazarsfeld, who first named the "personal influence" paradigm, codified it, and brought it to the center of the field, were explicitly aiming to dethrone the "hypodermic" theory.[15][29]

Gitlin proceeds to quote sections of two paragraphs from pages 16 and 17 of *Personal Influence*, which, as has been established, neither evoke a needle metaphor nor contain words such as *hypodermic* or *inject*. The corresponding endnotes are equally problematic. Endnote [14] reads as follows:

> For more on "personal influence" theory as a critique of the earlier "hypodermic" theory, see Elihu Katz, "Communication Research and the Image of Society: Convergence of Two Traditions," *American Journal of Sociology* 65 (March 1960), p. 113, and DeFleur, op. cit., pp. 112–117.[30]

Following the trail, we discover that page 113 of the *American Journal of Sociology*, Volume 65, is entirely occupied by a review of a book about leadership and power in Thailand.[31] Katz's article, which is found on pages 435–440 of the volume, contains no mention of *hypodermic* or related terms.[32] Pages 112–117 of the second edition of DeFleur's *Theories of Mass Communication* do not include a clear attribution of the label to Katz and Lazarsfeld, although *Personal Influence* is quoted.[33] Gitlin's endnote [15] refers us to pages 16 and 17 of *Personal Influence*, neither page of which contains the label.[34]

It is clear, after tracing each endnote to its source, that the quotation marks in question are meant to designate a coined expression rather than a direct quote. Gitlin clearly has the theory of direct and powerful effects, rather than the label *hypodermic*, in mind, but the distinction is not evident without following endnotes and checking sources. Furthermore, whatever else Gitlin's article may accomplish, it firmly establishes an association between *Personal Influence* and the hypodermic theory. In a span of two pages, *hypodermic* appears seven times, interspersed with "Katz and Lazarsfeld" and "personal influence." Given these circumstances, it is understandable how readers might close the pages of Gitlin's article thinking that Katz and Lazarsfeld coined *hypodermic*.

* * *

Harold Lasswell's *Propaganda* has sustained the same sort of punctuation-induced reputation as *Personal Influence*. The case of *Propaganda* is more complicated, however, because although Lasswell did not coin *hypodermic*, he did reference *injections* in the context of propaganda, and his propaganda research is generally considered an example of early work that assumed powerful, direct media influence.[35] Jesse G. Delia, for one, argues that *Propaganda* can be read as "an undifferentiated and direct-effects conception of mass communication," and Viekko Pietilä asserts that the notion of powerful media preying on defenseless victims is "present quite clearly" in this book.[36]

As is the case with *Personal Influence*, it is frequently difficult to distinguish between descriptions of Lasswell's work as an exemplification of the hypodermic *model* and accounts that name Lasswell's work as the source of the *label*. A textbook from the early 1980s, for example, states that "from Freudian theory Lasswell developed a theory labeled the *hypodermic-needle model* of mass communication because it assumed that media messages have direct effect, just as hypodermic needles inject their serum directly into the individual."[37] At first glance, this seems to be a clear attribution of the label to Lasswell, but an alternate interpretation—that Lasswell's theory was later labeled the "*hypodermic-needle model* of mass communication"—is also possible. This second reading is the one intended by the authors, who dropped the implied link to Lasswell in a later publication.[38] The ascription of the label to Lasswell in another textbook is also a case in point: "Lasswell (1935) suggested the 'hypodermic' model of media; that is, viewers were 'injected' with some dubious message that brought out their worst behavior and thoughts."[39] Suggesting a model is different than naming a model, but this statement is undeniably easy to read as an attribution of the label to Lasswell.

The above cases can be interpreted as references to the model rather than the label, but it is more difficult to derive alternate readings for a claim made by Ellen Wartella and Byron Reeves in a pivotal 1985 article on the history of research on children and media. Lasswell and the hypodermic model figure prominently in the first paragraph of the authors' recapitulation of the traditional—and, they argue, biased—history of media effects research.

> Earliest concerns about the mass media at the turn of the century and through the 1920s and early 1930s took the form of the direct effect or "hypodermic needle" model of media impact. The latter term, coined by political scientist Harold Lasswell during his analysis of World War I propaganda techniques, reflects an assumption that messages have a direct and undifferentiated impact on individuals.[40]

The traditional version of the field's history, Wartella and Reeves contend, incorporates work on public opinion, propaganda, public affairs, and voting, but fails to account for pre-1940s studies of children and media, notably those financed by the Payne Fund. In these studies, the authors observe, it is "difficult to find evidence of the 'hypodermic needle' model of media effects."[41]

That Lasswell coined the term is incidental to the larger themes of Wartella and Reeves's article. Yet the notion of Lasswell as the hypodermic label-maker remains a persistent, albeit peripheral, item in Wartella's later contributions to the field's history writing. In a 1991 article on the evolution of mass communication and persuasion models, Wartella, along with coauthor Susan Middlestadt, revises the earlier attribution of the term, writing that the hypodermic model was "articulated by Harold Lasswell in 1927."[42] A decade later, Wartella, this time with coauthor Patricia A. Stout, again attributes the label to Lasswell:

> The political scientist Harold Lasswell is said to have coined the phrase *the hypodermic needle model of media impact*, which captures the then dominant view about media's influence on audiences as having "direct effects." The effectiveness of the World War I propaganda campaigns (as studied by Lasswell, 1948), along with the rise of public relations during the first two decades of the century, with their ability to influence what newspapers printed about individuals and the ability of media to create the "pictures in our heads" as Walter Lippmann (1922) put it, created a sense of the enormous power of the mass media to directly influence their audiences.[43]

The 1948 article specified in Wartella and Stout's reference list does not address propaganda during World War I or any other period. It does, however, contain the classic articulation of the communicative act—"Who says what in which channel to whom with what effect?"—which can be interpreted as a simple, linear, and potentially hypodermic conceptualization of communication.[44]

The interchangeability of model and label is perhaps best demonstrated in the concluding chapter of a 1996 edited volume, *American Communication Research: The Remembered History*, in which Wartella addresses comments in an earlier article by Chaffee and Hochheimer. Wartella begins by identifying Lasswell as the source of the label: "The political scientist Harold Lasswell is said to have coined the term *hypodermic needle model* of media impact; this model, widely believed in this early period, held that the mass media have direct, powerful, and undifferentiated effects on audiences."[45] Several pages later, the distinction between the label and model begins to blur when Wartella remarks that "Steven H. Chaffee and J. L. Hochheimer (1985) reread Lasswell's work and found no evidence of use of the phrase *hypodermic needle* to refer to media effects."[46] In the article referenced, however, Chaffee and Hochheimer's own description of their methods is not so clearly laid out:

> Although it is Lasswell who is most often cited as the author of a "hypodermic needle" model of direct effects (e. g., Schramm, 1971; Davis and Baran, 1981; Dominick, 1983), it is difficult to find the evidence in his own writing. At most, this piece of imagery would have had a highly specific meaning in the context of Lasswell's essays of the 1930s.[47]

"It is difficult to find the evidence in [Lasswell's] own writing" is not necessarily the same as claiming to have reread *Propaganda* or Lasswell's other work in search of specific terms.[48] More importantly, it is not clear that Chaffee and Hochheimer are referring to the label, as opposed to merely the model. The phrase *piece of imagery* implies that Chaffee and Hochheimer have the metaphor of a hypodermic needle in mind, but an examination of the sources they cite indicates otherwise. Schramm, for one, promotes his own label, "Bullet Theory";[49] Davis and Baran likewise do not attribute the term *hypodermic* to Lasswell;[50] and Dominick does not mention Lasswell in the context of "the hypodermic approach."[51] Davis and Baran's statements, as discussed previously, are easy to misconstrue as an attribution of the label to Lasswell, but the references to Schramm and Dominick appear to be oversights on the part of Chaffee and Hochheimer. Both cases, however, can be explained as well within the bounds of *hypodermic*'s common usage in the field's literature, where injecting bullets and firing needles are generally not viewed as problematic.

* * *

That apocryphal stories of *hypodermic*'s coinage emerged through a combination of metaphor exchange, random acts of punctuation, and apparent instances of perfunctory attention to source citation (on the part of both writers and readers) makes for an explanation that is entertaining, but one that is, admittedly, incompletely reconstituted from published traces of the past. The answers to some questions undoubtedly remain in the lacunae of lectures, seminar discussions, verbal exchanges at conference panels, and the recesses of individual memory. What is puzzling is that the various stories of the label's origins coexist so unproblematically within widely distributed literature. As discussed in the following section, however, the model's slippery composition is key to the label's serviceability.

THOSE WHO WERE INFLUENCED: THE BELIEFS OF CRITICS, COMMENTATORS, AND PEOPLE

As Bineham has pointed out, there is no straightforward consensus as to what constitutes a hypodermic effect.[52] While searching for the first occurrence of *hypodermic* in the field's literature, I became increasingly aware that diverse, sometimes contradictory, conceptualizations of media influence are classified under the label. In an effort to sort out the various renditions of the model, I systematically recorded the basic features of hypodermic effects as described in more than 120 sources, with particular attention to descriptions of media influence and the identity of those purported to believe in hypodermic effects.[53] What follows is a summary of the hypodermic model constructed from the accounts in my sample.

If we limit the model's definition to those aspects of influence mentioned in a strict majority of the sources, we would be left with nothing but a debunked model from the past; however, a number of components are referred to in at least five percent of the sample. Direct and powerful effects are each found in almost half of the sources reviewed (49% and 45%, respectively), followed by uniformity of effect (20%) and immediacy of effect (15%). Audiences are characterized as helpless (24%), passive (21%), atomized (14%), and unreasoning (5%).[54] Fully equipped renditions of the model are relatively uncommon; in fact, almost one-third of the sample refers to the model by a single component, most often direct or powerful effects. Overall, descriptions of the hypodermic model emphasize features of media effects over audience characteristics; thirty-seven percent address only the effects of media, as compared to four percent that specify only audience characteristics. Finally, approximately twenty percent of the sample, primarily journal articles and book reviews, glosses over the model's composition entirely, opting instead to emphasize the model's defunct status with negative adjectives, such as *naïve, simplistic,* and *uncritical.*

To summarize, notions of what constitutes the hypodermic model vary widely, but this variation is not a cause for concern among communication researchers. Only one scholar in the reviewed sample takes issue with another's formulation of the model. DeFleur, in *Theories of Mass Communication,* expresses a preference for "mechanistic S-R theory"[55] over "hypodermic needle" and "transmission belt," because the latter "seem to overlook [the model's] basic underlying assumptions." He then contends that Katz and Lazarsfeld's rendition oversimplifies the model's structure by placing too much emphasis on the directness of media effects. "There were very definite assumptions about what was going on in between," DeFleur argues. "These assumptions may not have been explicitly formulated at the time, but they were drawn from fairly elaborate theories of human nature as well as the nature of the social order."[56] With the exception of DeFleur, however, the many renditions of what is labeled "hypodermic" coexist uncontested. Considering the sometimes heated tenor of debates involving other aspects of the model, this lack of contention over what constitutes a hypodermic effect is curious.

What *is* disputed, sometimes vehemently, is the matter of who believed (and in several cases, who currently believes) in hypodermic effects. The list of suspects is lengthy, ranging from motley collections of popular writers and commentators to communication researchers in general. Despite this diversity, it is a relatively straightforward matter to classify the accused according to the final "disposition" of each case.

First, there are the perpetrators who remain nameless—the "ones who get away" when writers manipulate sentence structure and voice to present the model as authorless and self-perpetuating. The following textbook elaboration of the "effects model" (which the authors equate with the "hypodermic model") uses passive voice to this effect:

> The language used in such writing will often imply that meanings are "injected" into this mass audience's minds by powerful, syringe-like media. The next step is often to describe the media as working like a drug, and then to suggest that the audience is drugged, addicted, doped or duped.[57]

Expunging *to be* and its conjugations from one's lexicon altogether would be nearly impossible—not to mention a waste of a perfectly useful verb—but in the above example, the authors use passive voice to avoid the issue entirely of who engages in "such writing." Personification is also frequently used to obscure the identities of those subscribing to notions of hypodermic effects. For example,

> Media impact tends to be misunderstood and often exaggerated because hypodermic theories remain rampant. According to these discredited theories, people exposed to messages adopt and interpret them exactly as presented, akin to media patients who are treated with a disease-specific vaccine.[58]

Here the hypodermic theories have managed to liberate themselves from their sources to exercise agency over unnamed (and presumably gullible) subjects. At a practical level, to prohibit theories from postulating and papers from arguing would fundamentally alter the nature of academic writing (for better or worse), but writers frequently use personification to evade the question of who believed in hypodermic effects.

When specific groups or individuals are charged with believing in hypodermic effects, advocates will, on occasion, emerge and attempt to introduce reasonable doubt. J. Michael Sproule, for example, moves to exempt interwar propaganda analysts from charges of simplistic speculation, arguing that their concern was with "the role of institutions in coloring communications given to the public" rather than the reception of messages by passive audiences.[59] Hypodermic allegations against the Payne Fund studies are disputed by Wartella and Reeves, whose view is seconded by Delia.[60] Werner J. Severin and James W. Tankard, Jr., accuse Jacques Ellul of harboring a "somewhat revised form" of the hypodermic model in *Propaganda: The Formation of Men's Attitudes*, but Francis Balle and Idalina Cappe de Baillon credit the same work with challenging "the relevance of the 'hypodermic needle' model as a representation of media effects."[61] Harold Lasswell, as discussed previously, is cited as believing in hypodermic effects, although Chaffee and Hochheimer cast doubt on this association.[62] The most frequently defended group by far, however, are communication researchers, although the specific constituents of this group are always subject to contextual interpretation. Indictments of communication researchers are relatively uncommon and are usually vague (the hypodermic model "permeated all different types of media theory and research")[63] and tempered by specifications of time ("earlier research on media effects")[64] or type ("some media sociologists").[65] Nevertheless, a number of writers insist that "no responsible communications researcher"—to borrow Gerbner's phrase—ever believed in hypodermic effects.[66]

Finally, some individuals and groups accused of believing in hypodermic effects go undefended. These include critics, essayists, observers, writers, commentators, religious leaders, political elites, theorists, scholars, academics, and members of the public. Some depictions of this group's constituents are decidedly unflattering ("the unsophisticated lay imagination looking for scapegoats"),[67] and members of this category are, on occasion, charged with still believing in hypodermic effects. Severin and Tankard, for example, are not alone in their observation that although the theory "has largely been discarded by mass communication researchers, it is apparently something that many people still believe."[68]

* * *

Although the wide variation in model composition is rarely questioned, the matter of *who* believed in hypodermic effects is highly contentious. This tolerance for definitional dissonance, alongside the persistent attempts to exculpate communication researchers, suggests that the label itself has less to do with the power of media or the vulnerability of audiences than with indicting those who ascribed (or still ascribe) to a hypodermic model of media influence. As I discuss below, the matter of who believed in hypodermic effects is key to understanding the "straw man's" resilience.

THE WORK OF REMEMBERING:
WHY THE STRAW MAN WON'T STAY BURIED

The three groups charged with hypodermic beliefs, then, are (1) those who get away, aided and abetted by passive voice and personification; (2) various individual scholars and communication researchers, all of whom are defended by their respective advocates; and (3) collections of undefended writers, theorists, and members of the general population. The first group's identity is, for obvious reasons, impossible to ascertain, but the latter two groups bear a striking resemblance to parties in a different drama played out in a neighboring field. Professional historians, John Nerone tells us, are ever alert to incursions by "other colonists"—theorists with their overarching narratives—and "barbarians"—members of the public with their uncritical proclivities. The primary means through which historians mount a defense of "history-land" against these invaders, Nerone suggests, is by emphasizing certain standards of scholarly practice.[69] In accounts of the hypodermic model, media scholars use similar means to distinguish their own work from that of other intellectuals ("other colonizers") and constituents of the popular mind ("barbarians"). Those who employ sophisticated ways of know-ing are defended; those who assume, speculate, conjecture, and believe are left to their own defenses. Sophistication is most often defined in terms of skill at wield-ing the tools of social science, but on occasion it is also associated with the acuity to step back and systematically assess the consequences as those tools are wielded. *Hypodermic* is not exclusive to the vocabulary of "administrative," "critical," or any other research faction.

Nowhere is this differentiation of the sophisticated from the unwitting more finely tuned than in an exchange between Steven Chaffee and Jeffrey Bineham in the September 1988 issue of *Communication Monographs*. Referencing an ear-lier article by Chaffee and Hochheimer as a key example,[70] Bineham observes that researchers who subscribe to the straw man argument—that the hypodermic model was constructed as a foil against which early limited effects research could be contrasted—restrict their evidence to empirical studies.[71] After emphatically agreeing with Bineham's point, Chaffee explains that the purpose of this restric-tion is to maintain "a fundamental disciplinary distinction that must be kept in mind if the history of the field in this century is to be understood."[72] Elsewhere in his response, Chaffee further elaborates this distinction:

> Applicants for graduate programs in mass communication, as yet unschooled but capable of synthesizing this body of common belief, fill their essays with assump-tions of massive media effects—as do politicians, critical theorists, columnists, and just about anyone who is given opportunity to express an opinion.[73]

The similarities between the groups listed by Chaffee, above, and the "people" and "certain schools of social science theory" of Katz's 1953 BASR report are not coincidental.[74] "Barbarians" and "other colonizers" are stock characters in "straw man" exposés as well as in accounts of the hypodermic model. Fundamental to both versions of the field's history is the question of who possesses legitimate ways of knowing and making claims about media, and in "straw man" exposés—the majority of which implicate the popular mind and critical scholars—this question is inevitably raised in the same breath in which the hypodermic model is demoted to a caricature. Lang's assertion (quoted earlier in the epigraph of this chapter) that the hypodermic theory "never really had any followers among persons we would consider social scientists" is followed by a clarification that the theory *was* "congruent with the popular fears" before moving on to a discussion of the theo-ry's use as a straw man.[75] Likewise, Gerbner transitions smoothly from contending that "no responsible communications researcher ever advanced a theory of help-less receivers falling under a hail of media bullets" to observing that the theory was advanced to "caricature exaggerated popular beliefs."[76] That media researchers (of whatever stripe) attempt to differentiate their own work from that of others who study, use, and make claims about media is no revelation, and neither is the use of the hypodermic model in emphasizing this distinction.[77] The crucial point of the present chapter is that "straw man" exposés serve the same differentiating function as the hypodermic model.

* * *

There is no simple answer to the question "Who said *hypodermic* first?" and it would be inaccurate to saddle a particular text or author with this "distinction." The earliest references to injections emphasize communicator influence over the part played by media. In many respects, Katz's BASR report is the best candidate, as it not only uses the term *hypodermic* to reference powerful media effects but shares telling characteristics with the vast majority of subsequent references to the hypodermic model. Notably, passive voice, personification, references to collective theorizing and research, and a dearth of citations conspire to make the identity of those believing in hypodermic effects difficult to define with any precision. Yet it is impossible to gauge the influence of a report that did not receive wide circulation. Perhaps collective "credit" is in order. Although it is inadvisable to speculate too freely about undocumented conversations and unpublished writing that may (or may not) have transpired more than fifty years ago, it is likely that the metaphor of a hypodermic needle was circulated among Bureau researchers, who went on to propagate the label. This explanation lends credence to the straw man argument made by Lang, Gerbner, Chaffee and Hochheimer, and others: the label was applied retroactively to a notion of media influence too extreme to be anything but a caricature, as a useful foil to the Bureau's "limited effects" findings.

But to bury the hypodermic model under the "straw man" epitaph is unsatisfactory and, if past attempts are accurate indicators, doomed to fail. Relegating the hypodermic model to straw man status has little effect on its function. Both stories—the hypodermic narrative of all-powerful media preying on a helpless audience, and the assertion that the hypodermic model is a straw man—serve the same purpose: to defend the territory of legitimate media scholarship from interlopers.

In light of the "straw man's" shifty constitution and active employment in warding off barbarians and other colonists, history may not be the best framework for thinking through the hypodermic model's function. To appropriate Pierre Nora's conceptualization, history is "the reconstruction, always problematic and incomplete, of what is no longer." The hypodermic model, clearly not in a state of "no longer," is better described as memory:

in permanent evolution, subject to the dialectic of remembering and forgetting, unconscious of the distortions to which it is subject, vulnerable in various ways to appropriation and manipulation, and capable of lying dormant for long periods only to be suddenly reawakened.[78]

Maintained through both overt boundary work and rhetorical grave-digging, the "straw man" survives because he is useful.

NOTES

1. The author wishes to thank Elihu Katz, Carolyn Marvin, Barbie Zelizer, Peter Simonson, Bill Herman, Sue Robinson, Paul Falzone, Bruce Hardy, and the Graduate Working Group in Communication and History at the Annenberg School for Communication for their valuable comments on earlier versions of this chapter.
2. "The European Roots," 6. Lang also addresses this topic in a review of the *Handbook of Political Communication*, 299–300, and in "Communications Research: Origins and Development," 374.
3. Chaffee and Hochheimer, "The Beginnings of Political Communication Research," 289–90.
4. Gerbner, "The Importance of Being Critical," 360.
5. Bineham, "A Historical Account of the Hypodermic Model in Mass Communication."
6. Berlo, *The Process of Communication*, 27.
7. For a brief history of the hypodermic needle's use in medicine, see Ghislaine, "The Hypodermic Syringe." For a comprehensive account, refer to Rosales, "A History of the Hypodermic Syringe."
8. Merton, *On the Shoulders of Giants*, 1–2. The resemblance of my own squirreling to Merton's—in the case of either *serendipity* or the allusion to standing on giants' shoulders—is one of spirit but not scale. By Merton's own account, he began accumulating references to the shoulders of giant's aphorism in 1942, more than twenty years before the book of the same name was published. See also Merton and Barber, *The Travels and Adventures of Serendipity*.
9. *Hypodermic* appears as early as 1926 in a journal read by secondary school language arts teachers with reference to the process of inculcating cultural taste in children. In an article prescribing a method for instilling "at least a fairly intelligent discrimination" in choice of reading material among high school students, Louise Drage of Rochester High School in Minnesota explains that "this knowledge of values is not to be attained in one day. It cannot be given in a concentrated dose or by hypodermic injection. It is a gradual process of assimilation; the result of sustained work on the part of the student" ("On the Use of Contemporary Literature," 539–40).
10. Lasswell, *Propaganda Technique in the World War*, 216–17. The role of mass media in administering the injection, although not specified by Lasswell in this example, can be inferred from his other elaborations of the function of news in circulating the symbols of propaganda.
11. "Influences of World Events on U.S. 'Neutrality' Opinion," 56. Jacob mentions radio, newsreel, and newspapers only in passing. His depiction of the influence of Roosevelt's speech as a "temporary hypodermic" is quoted by Gordon W. Allport and Janet M. Faden in the December 1940 issue of *Public Opinion Quarterly*. Whereas Jacob relies heavily on polling data and does not acknowledge the role of mass media in the formation of public opinion, Allport and Faden make inferences about public opinion from a content analysis of newspapers ("The Psychology of Newspapers," 700).
12. North, "A National Disgrace," 21.
13. Buswell, "Educational News and Editorial Comment," 333; Gray, "Educational News and Editorial Comment," 641–42; and Zorbaugh, "Editorial," 194.

14. Katz, "The Part Played by People," 6–7. For more on Katz's 1953 report, see Simonson, Introduction, 16–17. Simonson discovered the hypodermic needle reference in Katz's report and brought it to my attention.
15. In a later chapter of *Personal Influence*, Katz and Lazarsfeld do speak of the mass media being "injected" into interpersonal contexts, but the imagery of a hypodermic needle is not evoked. See *Personal Influence*, 133n20. For a discussion of the authorship of *Personal Influence*, see Pooley, "Fifteen Pages That Shook the Field," 149n1.
16. An analysis of journalism research conducted by Tankard, Jr., Chang, and Tsang named *Voting* as one of three "classics" of the field, alongside Klapper's *The Effects of Mass Communication* and Lazarsfeld, Berelson, and Gaudet's *The People's Choice* ("Citation Networks as Indicators of Journalism Research Activity").
17. Berelson, Lazarsfeld, and McPhee, *Voting*, 234.
18. "What We Know About the Effects of Mass Communication," 456. This is identical to Klapper's use of the term in *Effects of Mass Communication*, 5. In both publications, Klapper references *Voting* as the source of *hypodermic* and specifies the correct page number. James N. Druckman also references *Voting* with the correct page number ("The Implications of Framing Effects for Citizen Competence," 233).
19. *Process of Communication*, 27.
20. The bullets are sometimes of a "magic" or "silver" variety. Unlike *hypodermic*, the bullet metaphor's originator is relatively easy to identify, since Wilbur Schramm lays claim to this label ("The Nature of Communication between Humans," 8–9). However, as Paul Power, Robert Kubey, and Spiro Kiousis have pointed out, it is also feasible that the metaphor infiltrated the mass communication research literature via Lasswell's *Propaganda Technique in the World War* ("Audience Activity and Passivity," 125–26). In the final chapter of *Propaganda*, Lasswell quotes a U.S. military intelligence document that quotes George William Curtis as saying, "Thoughts are bullets" (214).
21. Biagi, *Media Impact*, 268; boldface type in original.
22. Stewart, Pavlou, and Ward, "Media Influences on Marketing Communications," 356.
23. "Fifteen Pages," 131. For more on the importance of *Personal Influence* in constructing the field's history, see Delia, "Communication Research: A History," 21; Pietilä, *On the Highway of Mass Communication Studies*, 2; and Schiller, *Theorizing Communication*, 42.
24. "What We Know," 456; *Effects of Mass Communication*, 5.
25. *Process of Communication*, 27–28.
26. "America, 'Mass Society,' and Mass Media," 6–9.
27. DeFleur, *Theories of Mass Communication*, 1st ed., 115.
28. Gitlin, "Media Sociology: The Dominant Paradigm"; Simonson, Introduction, 7–8.
29. "Media Sociology," 209–10.
30. Ibid., 247n14.
31. Apter, review of *Leadership and Power*.
32. Katz, "Communication Research and the Image of Society."
33. DeFleur, *Theories of Mass Communication*, 2nd ed., 112–17.
34. "Media Sociology," 247n15; *Personal Influence*, 16–17.
35. Lasswell's essay on "The Structure and Function of Communication in Society," published in Bryson, *The Communication of Ideas*, is also cited as the source of *hypodermic*, as is Lasswell, *World Politics and Personal Insecurity*. Like *Propaganda*, *World Politics* does reference injections, although not in relation to media effects (35, 216).

36. Delia, "Communication Research," 26; and Pietilä, *On the Highway of Mass Communication Studies*, 82. Chaffee and Hochheimer, however, question attributions of the hypodermic model to Lasswell; cf. "Beginnings of Political Communication Research," 285–86.

37. Davis and Baran, *Mass Communication and Everyday Life*, 25.

38. Baran and Davis, *Mass Communication Theory*, 66–69. In this later book, the *magic bullet* label is used in lieu of *hypodermic*. The authors' intent in the original publication was confirmed through correspondence (Dennis Davis, December 12, 2004).

39. Harris, *A Cognitive Psychology of Mass Communication*, 13. In the fourth edition of this textbook, Harris cites *Propaganda* alongside *World Politics and Personal Insecurity* as the source of this suggestion (21).

40. Wartella and Reeves, "Historical Trends in Research on Children and the Media," 118–19. More recently, Armand Mattelart and Michèle Mattelart have also attributed the label to Lasswell, using language similar to that of Wartella and Reeves: "The audience was seen as a passive target, blindly responding to stimuli. The media were thought to act like a 'hypodermic needle,' a term coined by Lasswell himself to designate their direct, undifferentiated impact on atomised individuals" (*Theories of Communication*, 26).

41. Wartella and Reeves, "Historical Trends," 122.

42. Wartella and Middlestadt, "The Evolution of Models of Mass Communication and Persuasion," 206.

43. Wartella and Stout, "The Evolution of Mass Media and Health Persuasion Models," 20–21.

44. Lasswell, "The Structure and Function of Communication in Society," 37. Although Lasswell's essay is widely recognized as the source of this model, Brett Gary argues that the model resulted from the collective efforts of researchers at the Rockefeller Foundation, as opposed to being the sole creation of Lasswell ("Communication Research, the Rockefeller Foundation").

45. Wartella, "The History Reconsidered," 169.

46. Ibid., 172.

47. "Beginnings of Political Communication Research," 286.

48. It should be noted, however, that Chaffee, in a related article, does make a claim of this sort for seven publications cited by Lazarsfeld, Berelson, and McPhee in *The People's Choice*. See "Differentiating the Hypodermic Model from Empirical Research," 247.

49. "Nature of Communication between Humans," 8–9.

50. *Mass Communication and Everyday Life*, 25.

51. Dominick, *The Dynamics of Mass Communication*, 404.

52. "A Historical Account of the Hypodermic Model," 239.

53. This number excludes references that use the label in passing with no further description or modification. A number of accounts that figure prominently in writing about the hypodermic model and the field's historiography in general do not use the term *hypodermic*. In addition to *Personal Influence*, notable examples are Bauer and Bauer, "America, 'Mass Society,' and Mass Media"; Curran, Gurevitch, and Woollacott, "The Study of the Media"; Czitrom, *Media and the American Mind*, 133–39; and Delia, "Communication Research." I collected the sample over several years, initially by backtracking through reference lists and later by conducting keyword searches in article databases, scouring the mass communication theory and methods sections of my university library, and ordering texts through interlibrary loan services. I am grateful to Joseph Turow, who generously granted access to his bookshelves during the early stages of research.

54. In calculating the frequency of each component, I included synonyms and equivalent phrases (e.g., "omnipotent" effects were counted as powerful). I also included components directly implied

by contrast with the limited effects model (e.g., that unlike the hypodermic model, more recent research has found that individuals respond differently to the same message).

55. "S-R" refers to "Sender-Receiver."
56. DeFleur, *Theories of Mass Communication*, 1st ed., 115.
57. Branston and Stafford, 403.
58. Graber, *Processing Politics*, 99.
59. See Sproule, "Progressive Propaganda Critics and the Magic Bullet Myth," 226.
60. Wartella and Reeves, "Historical Trends"; Delia, "Communication Research," 39–41. Jay Black and Jennings Bryant, on the other hand, write that the Payne Fund studies findings "appeared to be in line with the notion that mass media messages exercise powerful influences over passive, trusting, and vulnerable consumers" (*Introduction to Media Communication*, 53). David Glover also locates the Payne Fund studies among those based on a "hypodermic syringe model" (*The Sociology of the Mass Media*, 2–3).
61. Severin and Tankard, *Communication Theories*, 106; Ellul, *Propaganda*; Balle and Cappe de Baillon, "Mass Media Research in France," 150.
62. "Beginnings of Political Communication Research," 286.
63. Alexander and Jacobs, "Mass Communication, Ritual and Civil Society," 26.
64. Glynn and others, *Public Opinion*, 398.
65. Berger, *Essentials of Mass Communication Theory*, 111.
66. "Importance of Being Critical," 359.
67. Thelma McCormack, review of *Mass Communication*, 289.
68. *Communication Theories*, 247–48. In elaborating the category of "many people," the authors proceed to indict Pope John Paul II, a neurobiologist, a political scientist, and a dolphin expert.
69. Nerone, "Theory and History," 148–49. According to Nerone, historians stress objectivity, reject overarching narratives, and adhere to specified rules of argument. See also Gieryn on "boundary-work" ("Boundary-Work and the Demarcation of Science from Non-Science").
70. "Beginnings of Political Communication Research."
71. "A Historical Account of the Hypodermic Model," 238.
72. "Differentiating the Hypodermic Model from Empirical Research," 249.
73. Ibid., 248.
74. Katz, "Part Played by People," 6.
75. "European Roots," 6.
76. "Importance of Being Critical," 359.
77. Bineham's monograph addresses this point extensively ("A Historical Account of the Hypodermic Model").
78. Nora, "Between Memory and History," 3.

WORKS CITED

Alexander, Jeffrey C., and Ronald N. Jacobs. "Mass Communication, Ritual and Civil Society." In *Media, Ritual and Identity*, edited by Tamar Liebes and James Curran, 23–41. London: Routledge, 1998.

Allport, Gordon W., and Janet M. Faden. "The Psychology of Newspapers: Five Tentative Laws." *Public Opinion Quarterly* 4, no. 4 (1940): 687–703.

Apter, David E. Review of *Leadership and Power in the Chinese Community of Thailand*, by G. William Skinner. *American Journal of Sociology* 65, no. 1 (1959): 112–14.

Balle, Francis, and Idalina Cappe de Baillon. "Mass Media Research in France: An Emerging Discipline." *Journal of Communication* 33, no. 3 (1983): 146–56.

Baran, Stanley J., and Dennis K. Davis. *Mass Communication Theory: Foundations, Ferment, and Future.* Belmont, CA: Wadsworth, 1995.

Bauer, Raymond A., and Alice H. Bauer. "America, 'Mass Society,' and Mass Media." *Journal of Social Issues* 16, no. 3 (1960): 3–66.

Berelson, Bernard R., Paul F. Lazarsfeld, and William N. McPhee. *Voting: A Study of Opinion Formation in a Presidential Campaign.* Chicago: University of Chicago Press, 1954.

Berger, Arthur Asa. *Essentials of Mass Communication Theory.* Thousand Oaks, CA: Sage, 1995.

Berlo, David K. *The Process of Communication: An Introduction to Theory and Practice.* New York: Holt, Rinehart and Winston, 1960.

Biagi, Shirley. *Media Impact: An Introduction to Mass Media.* 7th ed. Belmont, CA: Wadsworth, 2005.

Bineham, Jeffery L. "A Historical Account of the Hypodermic Model in Mass Communication." *Communication Monographs* 55 (1988): 230–49.

Black, Jay, and Jennings Bryant. *Introduction to Media Communication.* 4th ed. Madison, WI: Brown and Benchmark, 1995.

Branston, Gill, and Roy Stafford. *The Media Student's Book.* 2nd ed. London: Routledge, 1999.

Buswell, G. T. "Educational News and Editorial Comment." *Elementary School Journal* 41, no. 5 (1941): 321–36.

Chaffee, Steven H. "Differentiating the Hypodermic Model from Empirical Research: A Comment on Bineham's Commentaries." *Communication Monographs* 55 (1988): 247–49.

Chaffee, Steven H., and John L. Hochheimer. "The Beginnings of Political Communication Research in the United States: Origins of the 'Limited Effects' Model." In *The Media Revolution in America and in Western Europe*, edited by Everett M. Rogers and Francis Balle, 267–96. Norwood, NJ: Ablex, 1985.

Curran, James, Michael Gurevitch, and Janet Woollacott. "The Study of the Media: Theoretical Approaches." In *Culture, Society and the Media*, edited by Michael Gurevitch, Tony Bennett, James Curran, and Janet Woollacott, 11–29. London: Routledge, 1982.

Czitrom, Daniel J. *Media and the American Mind: From Morse to McLuhan.* Chapel Hill: University of North Carolina Press, 1982.

Davis, Dennis K., and Stanley J. Baran. *Mass Communication and Everyday Life.* Belmont, CA: Wadsworth, 1981.

DeFleur, Melvin L. *Theories of Mass Communication.* 1st ed. New York: David McKay, 1966.

———. *Theories of Mass Communication.* 2nd ed. New York: David McKay, 1970.

Delia, Jesse G. "Communication Research: A History." In *Handbook of Communication Science*, edited by Charles R. Berger and Steven H. Chaffee, 20–98. Newbury Park, CA: Sage, 1987.

Dominick, Joseph R. *The Dynamics of Mass Communication.* Reading, MA: Addison-Wesley, 1983.

Drage, Louise. "On the Use of Contemporary Literature." *English Journal* 15, no. 7 (1926): 539–41.

Druckman, James N. "The Implications of Framing Effects for Citizen Competence." *Political Behavior* 23, no. 3 (2001): 225–56.

Ellul, Jacques. *Propaganda, the Formation of Men's Attitudes.* Translated by Konrad Kellen and Jean Lerner. New York: Knopf, 1965.

Gary, Brett. "Communication Research, the Rockefeller Foundation, and Mobilization for the War on Words, 1938–1944." *Journal of Communication* 46, no. 3 (1996): 124–47.

Gerbner, George. "The Importance of Being Critical—in One's Own Fashion." *Journal of Communication* 33, no. 3 (1983): 355–62.

Ghislaine, Lawrence. "The Hypodermic Syringe." *Lancet* 359, no. 9311 (2002): 1074.

Gieryn, Thomas F. "Boundary-Work and the Demarcation of Science from Non-Science: Strains and Interests in Professional Ideologies of Scientists." *American Sociological Review* 48 (1983): 781–95.

Gitlin, Todd. "Media Sociology: The Dominant Paradigm." *Theory and Society* 6, no. 2 (1978): 205–53.

Glover, David. *The Sociology of the Mass Media.* Ormskirk, Lancashire: Causeway Books, 1984.

Glynn, Carroll J., Susan Herbst, Garrett J. O'Keefe, and Robert Y. Shapiro. *Public Opinion.* Boulder, CO: Westview Press, 1999.

Graber, Doris A. *Processing Politics: Learning from Television in the Internet Age.* Chicago: University of Chicago Press, 2001.

Gray, William S. "Educational News and Editorial Comment." *Elementary School Journal* 42, no. 9 (1942): 641–55.

Harris, Richard Jackson. *A Cognitive Psychology of Mass Communication.* Hillsdale, NJ: Lawrence Erlbaum, 1989.

———. *A Cognitive Psychology of Mass Communication.* 4th ed. Mahwah, NJ: Lawrence Erlbaum, 2004.

Jacob, Philip E. "Influences of World Events on U.S. 'Neutrality' Opinion." *Public Opinion Quarterly* 4, no. 1 (1940): 48–65.

Katz, Elihu. "The Part Played by People: A New Focus for the Study of Mass Media Effects." Bureau Report B-0482-3. New York: Bureau of Applied Social Research, 1953.

———. "Communication Research and the Image of Society: Convergence of Two Traditions." *American Journal of Sociology* 65, no. 5 (1960): 435–40.

Katz, Elihu, and Paul F. Lazarsfeld. *Personal Influence: The Part Played by People in the Flow of Mass Communications.* Glencoe, IL: Free Press, 1955.

Klapper, Joseph T. "What We Know About the Effects of Mass Communication: The Brink of Hope." *Public Opinion Quarterly* 21, no. 4 (winter 1957–1958): 453–74.

———. *The Effects of Mass Communication.* New York: Free Press of Glencoe, 1960.

Lang, Kurt. "Communications Research: Origins and Development." In *International Encyclopedia of Communications*, Vol. 1, edited by Erik Barnouw, George Gerbner, Wilbur Schramm, Tobia L. Worth, and Larry Gross, 369–74. New York: Oxford University Press, 1989.

———. "The European Roots." In *American Communication Research: The Remembered History*, edited by Everette E. Dennis and Ellen Wartella, 1–20. Mahwah, NJ: Lawrence Erlbaum, 1996.

———. Review of *Handbook of Political Communication*, edited. by Dan D. Nimmo and Keith R. Sanders. *Public Opinion Quarterly* 47, no. 2 (1983): 297–300.

Lasswell, Harold D. *Propaganda Technique in the World War.* New York: Alfred A. Knopf, 1927.

———. "The Structure and Function of Communication in Society." In *The Communication of Ideas*, edited by Lyman Bryson, 37–51. New York: Institute for Religious and Social Studies, 1948.

———. *World Politics and Personal Insecurity.* New York: McGraw-Hill, 1935.

Lazarsfeld, Paul, Bernard Berelson, and Hazel Gaudet. *The People's Choice: How the Voter Makes up His Mind in a Presidential Campaign.* New York: Duell, Sloan and Pearce, 1944.

Mattelart, Armand, and Michèle Mattelart. *Theories of Communication: A Short Introduction.* Translated by Susan Gruenheck Taponier and James A. Cohen. London: Sage, 1998.

McCormack, Thelma. Review of *Mass Communication: A Sociological Perspective*, by Charles R. Wright. *Contemporary Sociology* 5, no. 3 (1976): 288–89.

Merton, Robert K. *On the Shoulders of Giants: A Shandean Postscript,* Vicennial ed. San Diego, CA: Harcourt Brace Jovanovich, 1985.

Merton, Robert K., and Elinor Barber. *The Travels and Adventures of Serendipity: A Study in Sociological Semantics and the Sociology of Science*. Princeton, NJ: Princeton University Press, 2004.

Nerone, John. "Theory and History." *Communication Theory* 3, no. 2 (1993): 148–57.

Nora, Pierre. "Between Memory and History." In *Realms of Memory: The Construction of the French Past*. Vol. 1 *Conflicts and Divisions*. Edited by Lawrence D. Kritzman, translated by Arthur Goldhammer, under the direction of Pierre Nora, 1–20. New York: Columbia University Press, 1996.

North, Sterling. "A National Disgrace." *Chicago Daily News*, May 8, 1940, 21.

Pietilä, Veikko. *On the Highway of Mass Communication Studies*. Cresskill, NJ: Hampton Press, 2005.

Pooley, Jefferson. "Fifteen Pages That Shook the Field: *Personal Influence*, Edward Shils, and the Remembered History of Mass Communication Research." In "Politics, Social Networks, and the History of Mass Communications Research: Rereading *Personal Influence*," edited by Peter Simonson, special issue. *Annals of the American Academy of Political and Social Science* 608 (2006): 130–56.

Power, Paul, Robert Kubey, and Spiro Kiousis. "Audience Activity and Passivity: An Historical Taxonomy." In *Communication Yearbook 26*, edited by William B. Gudykunst, 116–59. Mahwah, NJ: Lawrence Erlbaum, 2002.

Rosales, Patricia Ann. "A History of the Hypodermic Syringe, 1850's–1920's." PhD diss., Harvard University, 1998.

Schiller, Dan. *Theorizing Communication: A History*. New York: Oxford University Press, 1996.

Schramm, Wilbur. "The Nature of Communication between Humans." In *The Process and Effects of Mass Communication*, edited by Wilbur Schramm and Donald F. Roberts, 3–53. Rev. ed. Urbana: University of Illinois Press, 1971.

Severin, Werner J., and James W. Tankard, Jr. *Communication Theories: Origins, Methods, and Uses in the Mass Media*. 3rd ed. New York: Longman, 1992.

Simonson, Peter. Introduction to "Politics, Social Networks, and the History of Mass Communications Research: Rereading *Personal Influence*," edited by Peter Simonson, special issue. *Annals of the American Academy of Political and Social Science* 608 (2006): 6-24.

Sproule, J. Michael. "Progressive Propaganda Critics and the Magic Bullet Myth." *Critical Studies in Mass Communication* 6, no. 3 (1989): 225–46.

Stewart, David W., Paulos Pavlou, and Scott Ward. "Media Influences on Marketing Communications." In *Media Effects: Advances in Theory and Research*, 2nd ed., edited by Jennings Bryant and Dolf Zillmann, 353–96. Mahwah, NJ: Lawrence Erlbaum, 2002.

Tankard, James W., Jr., Tsan-Kuo Chang, and Kuo-Jen Tsang. "Citation Networks as Indicators of Journalism Research Activity." *Journalism Quarterly* 61, no. 1 (1984): 89–96.

Wartella, Ellen. "The History Reconsidered." In *American Communication Research: The Remembered History*, edited by Everette E. Dennis and Ellen Wartella, 169–80. Mahwah, NJ: Lawrence Erlbaum, 1996.

Wartella, Ellen, and Byron Reeves. "Historical Trends in Research on Children and the Media: 1900–1960." *Journal of Communication* 35, no. 2 (1985): 118–33.

Wartella, Ellen, and Patricia A. Stout. "The Evolution of Mass Media and Health Persuasion Models." In *Mass Media and Drug Prevention: Classic and Contemporary Theories and Research*, edited by William D. Crano and Michael Burgoon, 19–34. Mahwah, NJ: Lawrence Erlbaum, 2002.

Wartella, Ellen, and Susan Middlestadt. "The Evolution of Models of Mass Communication and Persuasion." *Health Communication* 3, no. 4 (1991): 205–15.

Zorbaugh, Harvey. "Editorial." *Journal of Educational Sociology* 18, no. 4 (1944): 193–94.

CHAPTER TWO

THE New History OF Mass Communication Research

JEFFERSON POOLEY

The full story of mass communications research still waits to be written.

—R. L. Brown (1970)[1]

Until recently, the extant literature on the history of mass communication research has been notoriously sparse, celebratory, and methodologically naïve. This chapter traces, and attempts to explain, a marked shift in that history over the past decade—from an airbrushed and unapologetically Whiggish rendering of the field's past to a rigorous, contextualist treatment with an altogether different story to tell.

This eruption of revisionist history resembles, in many respects, the historiographical self-scrutiny of other social science disciplines. The chapter's title, indeed, is an allusion to Robert Alun Jones's classic paper on "The New History of Sociology." That essay was published in 1983, and it documents a decade-long surge of accomplished historical work informed, Jones shows, by an engagement with Thomas Kuhn, Quentin Skinner, and debates in the history and sociology of science. Although the timing and contours varied by discipline, the other social sciences all experienced similar waves of critical historiography, beginning in the late 1960s or, more often, the early 1970s. By the early 1980s, when Jones wrote his survey, each discipline—sociology, political science, anthropology, and psychology—had attracted a small community of serious historians with, in many cases, subdisciplinary trappings like journals, archives, and divisional status within their fields' scholarly associations. These "new history" subdisciplines, owing to their post-Kuhnian intellectual coordinates and newly won autonomy, each produced a set of studies that lanced their discipline's self-serving origin myths.

These "new histories" emerged from the much broader tumult that had been reverberating around the social sciences since the late 1960s. This complex and overdetermined unrest reflected flagging confidence in the postwar social scientific elite, with its cocksure scientism, cold war liberalism, and federal government entanglements. Across the social sciences, youthful insurgent-scholars highlighted the gap between postwar social scientists' self-description as neutral observers, and their actual works' implicit support for the status quo. Self-identified radical factions formed in most of the social sciences, linked to the student New Left. This political radicalism overlapped, though unevenly, with a methodological backlash against pretensions to natural science status—often branded with the loose catchall "positivism"—in favor of various reflexive theories of knowledge.

The discipline-by-discipline leftist insurrection, together with the wars over method, lay the groundwork for the "new history" in a straightforward way: the effort to show that their disciplines' scientistic and progressivist self-descriptions were false required historical counter-narratives. In a related sense, the genealogical impulse was helped along by the state of upheaval itself—self-scrutiny often follows the disruption of taken-for-granted disciplinary norms. The skeptical and contextualist turn within the sociology and history of science fields, which reflected and contributed to the wider tumult, also fed the "new historians'" challenge to textbook fables and graduate seminar yarns.

Communication research experienced its own, now-notorious "ferment," albeit a few years later.[2] Many of the same political and methodological currents coursed through the communication research of the period. But unlike the other social sciences, there was, for communication, no real historiographical counterpart to the discipline's own "critical turn." There was some critical history, to be sure—exemplified by Todd Gitlin's 1978 "Media Sociology: The Dominant Paradigm." But Gitlin and other critical researchers largely adopted the standard history of the field, though that history was recast in negative terms. These were thinly sourced polemics, and not the kind of rigorous histories that Jones labeled "new."

This chapter asks the question: why did mass communication research fail to produce a body of contextualist history until the mid-1990s—more than twenty years late?

THE HISTORY OF COMMUNICATION RESEARCH, OLD AND NEW

Communication study in the United States, jury-rigged from the scraps of journalism schools and speech departments in the years following World War II, has from the beginning suffered from a legitimacy deficit. The would-be discipline, in its newly institutionalized form, was flush with the resources that other, more established disciplines covet—research funds, students, and faculty jobs, all in abundance. But the field lacked legitimacy, and this threatened all of its material riches. Communication studies scrambled to justify its very existence—faced, as it was, with a kind of cultural lag. Its institutional gains had far outpaced its status.[3]

A body of disciplinary history was drafted, in the early 1960s, to carry some of this legitimacy burden—at least for that portion of the discipline that evolved from journalism schools. (It is an index of the field's schizophrenia that the speech- and journalism-derived traditions have developed distinct disciplinary histories, both of which, however, claim to represent the field as a whole.)[4] The mass communication field, busy colonizing journalism schools, had mnemonic entrepreneurs like Wilbur Schramm who took scraps of memory lying about in the postwar social scientific landscape, and assembled these into a coherent, and self-validating, narrative. This history was translated into a standard textbook formula soon after, and propagated without serious challenge for decades. Students of communication studies well into the 1990s were reared on its plot. Most still are, today.

The standard history has two strands, one lifted from postwar media sociology and the other self-consciously narrated by Schramm. The first was constructed by sociologists, notably Paul F. Lazarsfeld, affiliated with the Bureau of Applied Social Research (BASR) at Columbia University—who created a rather flimsy but exceptionally durable straw man with which to contrast themselves. The Bureau researchers, as crystallized in the enormously influential account offered in the first chapter of Elihu Katz and Lazarsfeld's culminating work, *Personal Influence*, presented their prewar scholarly predecessors as naïve, impressionistic, uninformed amateurs who mistakenly clung to a "hypodermic needle" or "magic bullet" theory of media influence—and who, what's more, were under the spell of European "mass society theory," itself an influential straw man construct.[5] This remarkably resilient caricature of prewar influence was contrasted with the scientific, methodologically sophisticated (and reassuring) "limited effects" conclusions of the Bureau.[6]

The second strand was a self-conscious creation of Schramm, a consummate academic entrepreneur who was almost single-handedly responsible for the mass communication field's institutionalization.[7] First elaborated in 1963, Schramm's genealogy credits the discipline's plucky emergence to four pioneers—"founding fathers," he labels them.[8] The text, though, renders the anointment in the passive voice ("Four men have usually been considered the 'founding fathers'. . .")—an act of audacious creativity that comes off as mere reportage.[9] Kurt Lewin, Carl Hovland, Harold Lasswell, and Lazarsfeld himself—two psychologists, a political scientist, and a sociologist, all eminent bearers of scholarly capital—are invoked as predisciplinary forerunners of communication studies. Schramm's was a kind of involuntary draft: though these figures worked on "communication"-related problems at least occasionally, none would recognize himself in Schramm's communication pantheon—each had either died or moved on to other questions by 1963. Still, here they are; and if these four giants left distinct lineages, then happily their boundaries have since become porous: "These four strands of influence are still visible in communication research in the United States," writes Schramm, "but increasingly they have tended to merge."[10] Current "practitioners," for example, conduct "quantitative, rather than speculative" research—a legacy of the four founders.[11]

Like the account offered up by Katz and Lazarsfeld, Schramm's founders story is taut and Whiggish. The essay, which he was to publish in revised form at least five more times over the next three decades, is an unabashed origin myth.[12] It is neither history nor systematics, but something cartoonish in between—legitimacy on loan. The essay contains not a single footnote; its focus on convergence and recent institutional gains would make Herbert Butterfield blush. And like the *Personal Influence* history, Schramm's narrative was embraced by an insecure and newly institutionalized field.

By the mid-1960s, the two chronicles had merged, awkwardly, to form a single mnemonic stream: a powerful-to-limited-effects emplotting, welded to an equally upbeat forerunner-to-maturity narrative. Together, Katz, Lazarsfeld, and Schramm had furnished mass communication studies with a disciplinary memory—with a past that was eminently usable. The storyline supplied glue to a field with bricks but no mortar.

A challenge to this standard history did emerge in the 1970s and early 1980s, mounted by various "critical" strands of media research then ascendant. These critical currents, taken together, roughly paralleled the upheaval of the other social sciences in this period. But those other social sciences produced sophisticated revisionist history and emergent subdisciplinary communities; mass communication research did not. Indeed, the historical rethinking ushered in by the field's critical upsurge is notable for its embrace of the standard storylines—which are merely renarrated in a muckraking mold, but left otherwise intact.[13]

The agenda-setting text in the critical narrative was Todd Gitlin's 1978 "Media Sociology: The Dominant Paradigm," a scathing dismissal of the Lazarsfeld legacy and its "limited effects" conclusions. Gitlin attributed the Lazarsfeld circle's "limited effects" conclusions to its dependence on market research and especially media firm sponsorship, on the theory that Lazarsfeld and his Bureau colleagues were telling the media barons what they wanted to hear, that mass media exposure is harmless. Though the essay has other problems,[14] the crucial misstep is that it accepted Katz and Lazarsfeld's own *Personal Influence* self-description—and their "powerful effects" contrast too—so that his account rests on rickety and misleading foundations from the start. Katz and Lazarsfeld, wrote Gitlin,

> conceptualize the audience as a tissue of interrelated individuals rather than as isolated point-targets in a mass society ... As a corrective to overdrawn 'hypodermic' notions, as a reinstatement of society within the study of social communication, the new insistence on the complexity of the mediation process made good sense.[15]

Gitlin reproduced the mythical "hypodermic needle" periodizing, and also the Katz and Lazarsfeld tradition's self-description as pioneers of the "limited effects" finding. He merely adds a third stage, in terms evocative of the Christian typology of Eden, the fall, and the second coming: Lazarsfeld's limited effects as a necessary interregnum before a higher and better critical paradigm emerged. Here history is being used as a weapon in paradigmatic succession. Though there are hints of an externalist sociology of knowledge approach, there is in Gitlin's influential paper very little actual historical digging.

Many of the highly charged essays in the "Ferment in the Field" special issue of the *Journal of Communication* (1983) made historical claims akin to (and often rooted in) Gitlin's account. Here again, the treatments largely mirrored the mainstream narrative, which is set up as an easily toppled contrast to emerging critical researchers.[16] So too with the nascent 1970s British sociology and cultural studies of media, which constructed *its* identity against the "American effects tradition."[17]

In the same period, a number of notable attempts at retelling the story of the field's origins, in whole or in part, were made outside of these critical currents. Kurt and Gladys Lang, Willard Rowland, David Morrison, Daniel Czitrom, and Jesse Delia: each drafted more or less serious accounts of the discipline's history, yielding some genuinely new insights. But these histories, too, stopped short of challenging the "limited effects" storyline that Katz and Lazarsfeld had so effectively narrated.[18]

ENTER THE NEW HISTORY

In the late 1980s and early 1990s, a new, growing body of critical history began to undermine the received narrative. This barbed, debunking history replaced the older version's internalist methods and progressive narrative with a robustly externalist approach. Drawing on the archives of the Rockefeller Foundation, on the files and letters of key postwar figures including Wilbur Schramm and Paul Lazarsfeld, and on various materials from the National Archives and documents secured through the Freedom of Information Act, this cluster of "new historians" constructed an alternative narrative of communication study's genesis—one that stresses the conditioning role of Rockefeller, military, Central Intelligence Agency (CIA), and State Department funding, and also the tight interpersonal network of future communication scholars that coalesced during their common wartime government employment as overseas and domestic propagandists.[19]

There are six figures, with diverse backgrounds from American studies to the sociology of knowledge, who have stitched this new history together: Christopher Simpson, an investigative journalist; Timothy Glander, an education professor; Rohan Samarajiva, a development communication scholar; Brett Gary, a professional historian; William Buxton, a German-trained sociologist of knowledge; and J. Michael Sproule, whose roots are in speech communication. The six scholars, with an accidental and fortuitous division of historical labor, chronicle the emergence and consolidation of the mainstream effects tradition, in ways that differ strikingly from the dominant narratives I trace above.

Their histories tend to be methodologically reflective, though they distinguish themselves most by their archival digging; in contrast to earlier narrators of the field's past, the new historians have dirtied their fingernails. What they have dug up is that the mainstream effects tradition was crucially shaped, in the mid-1930s, by the Rockefeller Foundation's interest, first, in educational broadcasting and, after 1939, in anti-Nazi propaganda. The social scientists involved in this Rockefeller-funded effort, according to the new historians, formed the nucleus of the massive propaganda and "psychological warfare" bureaucracy set up in World War II. The new historians argue that, with much the same overlapping group of scholars, and with the wartime effort's infrastructural remnants, mass communication research matured in the early cold war. In a startling and incendiary conclusion, the new historians—notably Simpson and Glander—make the case that postwar media research was organized around the search for effective propaganda design on behalf of its State Department, military, and CIA funders. This is, of course, a long way from Katz and Lazarsfeld's self-professed "limited effects" finding. And the new historians' narrative doesn't just contradict the mainstream story, but also critical scholars' account of the field's past.

It is easy to paint with too broad a brush here: The six scholars differ in a number of important ways, and they would not all embrace the counternarrative, in its entirety, that I outline above. There is also a tonal and evaluative contrast worth stressing: Simpson and Glander, for example, tend to explicitly condemn the field's dalliance with government-funded propaganda, while Gary and Sproule are more forgiving. Though the six share a "family resemblance" in Wittgenstein's sense, there is a striking absence of cross-citation and other evidence of collaboration. The continuity I trace here is by ascription, in other words, and might not be recognized by those it describes.

THE INTERWAR YEARS: JOHN MARSHALL
AND THE ROCKEFELLER FOUNDATION

Buxton, Sproule, and Gary focus on the 1930s and the emergence of the mainstream "effects" tradition. Their histories, in line with many standard accounts, highlight the importance of Paul Lazarsfeld's Office of Radio Research (ORR), established in 1936 with funding from the Rockefeller Foundation.[20] Unlike previous accounts, however, the new history reconstructs in detail the context around that Rockefeller intervention. In particular, the foundation's John Marshall—who had been the most neglected major figure in the historiography of mass communication research—emerges as a key protagonist.

Buxton, a sociologist of knowledge who wrote a notable, somewhat muckraking study of Talcott Parsons in the 1980s,[21] provides the richest treatment of the foundation's early 1930s involvement in then-heated debates over commercial and educational radio.[22] Buxton's research is the most informed about the existing historiography of the field, which he masterfully critiques.[23] Gary, an intellectual historian, charts the immediate prewar years in terms of "nervous" liberal intellectuals and their Rockefeller-organized effort to promote intervention and plan a propaganda defense against the Nazis before it was politically palatable for the Roosevelt administration.[24] In an earlier essay, he presents an excellent, compact treatment of the Rockefeller role in organizing the "Communications Seminar" in the lead-up to the U.S. entry to war.[25] Sproule, finally, is a speech communication scholar who has mounted a multiyear project to recover the forgotten "propaganda analysis" paradigm which, as he details in a number of fascinating essays and a recent book, was self-consciously pushed aside in the Rockefeller-sponsored prewar propaganda mobilization.[26] Without any coordination, their research is nevertheless complementary, and together they provide a remarkably coherent picture of the foundation's formative role.

The Rockefeller investment in radio research, as Buxton details, was an outgrowth of its involvement in the public debate over educational radio—the so-called radio wars of 1927 to 1934, when federal communications policy was in flux. The debate—its factions and the ultimate outcome—set the initial parameters for the foundation's subsequent radio research programs, Buxton shows.

After the anarchic and interference-plagued airwaves of the 1920s had been brought under initial federal control with the 1927 Radio Act, a vigorous public debate broke out. Educational broadcasters, in particular, worried that the Act's new technical standards would drive out noncommercial stations.[27] There was, as Buxton describes in detail, a critical split in the educational camp—between a moderate group backed by John D. Rockefeller, Jr., and the Carnegie Corporation, and a less conciliatory group funded by a small Payne Fund grant. The Rockefeller-backed group urged cooperation between the networks and reformers, and proposed to develop high-quality educational programs that commercial broadcasters would find attractive. The Payne-backed group set out, instead, to lobby Congress and build public support for a fixed-percentage spectrum set-aside.[28] The 1934 Communication Act that emerged from the legislative and public battles was, of course, a victory for the commercial broadcasters, which included no mandated set-aside. But the Act did gesture toward the "public interest," and the new Federal Communications Commission (FCC) called a meeting to reconcile differences between the educators and the broadcasters, which ended in further acrimony.[29]

Buxton documents how the Rockefeller Foundation's interest in the study of radio emerged from the meeting and its bitter aftermath. The Foundation's Humanities Division (HD) essentially took over the government's underfunded effort to achieve a reconciliation.[30] John Marshall, the HD assistant director, played the key role in this and other communication-related Rockefeller initiatives.[31] After the post-Act meeting, he interviewed the main players in the debate, including broadcasters. As his diaries reveal, he came to share the moderate group's belief that commercial and educational goals were ultimately reconcilable.[32] Accepting commercial radio as a given—indeed, largely adopting the Rockefeller-backed moderate group's stance—Marshall sought to convince the networks to voluntarily embrace some educational programming.[33] The Foundation, in this vein, funded fellowship appointments at NBC and CBS to train public broadcasters.[34] But Marshall, by 1936, came to believe that only objective audience data would persuade the networks that some educational programming is in their interests.

It was Hadley Cantril, then an ambitious, thirty-year-old psychologist, who convinced Marshall that polling techniques, newly prominent after the infamous *Literary Digest* upset, could yield valuable data on audience interests and motivations. Cantril, then at Columbia's Teachers College, had recently published *The Psychology of Radio* (1935) with his Harvard mentor Gordon Allport. As Marshall later recalled in an oral history interview cited by Buxton, the "historic moment" came when he read Allport and Cantril's book—based mostly in experimental laboratory studies, but including some survey data—which in its conclusion urged that more research be conducted on listeners.[35]

When Marshall interviewed him, Cantril invoked the polling procedures and proposed to Marshall that he, Cantril, conduct laboratory and sampling-based research into listener tastes.[36] (Cantril had been serving on a committee, formed in early 1936 by the FCC to mediate between educators and broadcasters, which Marshall was closely following.) Impressed, Marshall urged Cantril to submit a request for funding; his initial proposal called for ongoing research into "what listeners find of interest in radio programs and . . . why these interests exist"—research, he argued, that would not be trusted if it emanated from either the broadcasters or the educators.[37]

A series of complicated maneuvers followed—which Buxton documents— that resulted in Cantril's revised proposal, this time with CBS's Frank Stanton as a partner, for a radio research bureau, which Marshall openly supported.[38] In his statement to the Rockefeller trustees, Marshall framed the research center as the key to bringing the broadcasters around to educational programming:

> If the present project succeeds, as I expect it will, in demonstrating the feasibility and significance of studying the actual and potential public service of radio to its total audience, it will set a style which the broadcasters cannot afford to disregard.[39]

In early 1937, the trustees approved a grant of $67,000 over two years to fund a "Princeton Radio Research Project," whose charter explicitly forbade research that questioned the commercial basis of the broadcasting.[40] It was Marshall who arranged that the Project be located at Princeton, and he seems to have played the crucial role in securing a post for Cantril in the University's psychology department. At around the same time, Cantril became one of the founding editors of the Princeton-based *Public Opinion Quarterly*—which the foundation also funded.[41]

When the Radio Project grant was awarded, Stanton was designated director, with Cantril as associate director. But Stanton, as he later recalled, was so "completely involved in what [he] was doing at CBS" that he declined to leave the network.[42] Cantril, too, was unwilling to assume the directorship, and the pair went looking for an appropriate candidate by asking around in psychological and sociological circles, and settled on Paul Lazarsfeld.[43] Though the Foundation was initially reluctant—concerned, as Marshall recalled later, that Lazarsfeld's interests were too broad—the appointment was made. The Rockefeller Foundation's expressed desire to get educational programming on commercial radio had, through this circuitous route, issued in the Office of Radio Research. Lazarsfeld's ORR (later the Bureau of Applied Social Research at Columbia) would proceed, of course, to help set the field's intellectual and methodological agenda during and after the war.

As Buxton, Sproule, and especially Gary document in great detail, the Foundation's next venture into media research was motivated on entirely different grounds, with arguably more lasting consequences for the communication field. With the rapid Nazi conquest of continental Europe as backdrop, Marshall in 1939 organized a "Communications Seminar" that was, in effect, a self-conscious precursor to the government propaganda campaigns of the war— convened in the knowledge that explicit government efforts, at that time, were not politically feasible.[44] One of the outcomes of the Seminar was the consolidation of the "communications" label itself, which as Sproule details was put forward as a deliberate alternative to the "propaganda analysis" tradition—whose Progressive emphasis on propaganda inoculation, in the new context of intervention and defense against the Nazis, risked obscuring the crucial distinction between (German) propaganda and (American) morale building.[45] Many of the Seminar participants—including Lazarsfeld, Cantril, and Harold Lasswell—would go on to leading roles in the government's wartime propaganda activities. As it evolved, the Seminar came to define the study of mass communications in largely quantitative terms, and identified the question of media effects as its driving problem. As both Sproule and Gary document, the field of communication was conceived in the Seminar as both an emerging scientific field and as a crucial instrument of effective propaganda design.[46]

The Seminar—a truly fascinating episode in the sociology of knowledge— was initially conceived by Marshall in terms of his interest in media study as a potential bridge-building between educators and commercial broadcasters. In late 1938, he proposed, to the Rockefeller trustees, a series of conferences centered on the prospects for the public's media-led education.[47] In August 1939, just before the outbreak of war, the foundation agreed to fund the series, which, in the proposal's language, was designed to develop a disciplined approach to the study of mass communication, through such media as radio, motion pictures, and print." One of its explicit charges was to identify a "general body of theory about mass communications in American culture.[48]

Before the first conference—the meetings only later came to be called the "Communications Seminar" or, less often, the "Communications Group"—the Nazi conquest of Central Europe was already underway. The Seminar's work over the following two years was forged by two competing, but ultimately merged, agendas: to map out the scientific study of mass communication, and to design an extragovernmental plan for combating Nazi propaganda and mobilizing war support. Most of the Seminar members, at least by 1940, had come to adopt a robustly scientistic view of communication research that was, significantly, also conceived as a major weapon in the world struggle.[49] Sproule has aptly labeled this seemingly schizophrenic scientific instrumentalism as an "ideology of service and science."[50] Before this rough consensus was formed, however, the Seminar's debates split along two axes that were not, moreover, clearly parallel to one another. Some of the participants were resistant to the others' stress on quantitative techniques. Along another axis, Seminar members disagreed about whether media research should be used for propaganda design. In the end, as Gary and Sproule show, the group's momentum and the developments in Europe brought most of the members together in recommending a quantitatively oriented science of propaganda design.

The Seminar issued its first group report in July 1940, "Research in Mass Communications," which laid out the famous "*who* says *what* in which *channel* to *whom* with what *effect*" formulation—which, however, has long been credited solely to Lasswell, probably because this initial, group formulation was kept secret.[51] The report's collective call for war-related opinion management was unambiguous:

> We believe . . . that for leadership to secure that consent will require unprecedented knowledge of the public mind and of the means by which leadership can secure consent. . . . We believe. . . . that we have available today methods of research which can reliably inform us about the public mind and how it is being, or can be, influenced in relation to public affairs.[52]

The Seminar's early ambivalence and qualifications were missing from the report, and some members openly decried its "fascistic" implications.[53] In response to the complaints, the group's final report, issued in October, was far less brazen in its language and recommendations. Titled "Needed Research in Communication," the document called for "two-way communication" between the government and the people; without it, the report warned, "democracy is endangered." The report concedes that the new mass communication research might be used for propagandistic ends, but asserts that such "authoritarian" cooptation could and should be avoided.[54]

The document's disclaimers, however, are more than a little disingenuous, as the foundation was already building an elaborate network of propaganda-related research projects, in lieu of a government-directed campaign. At the Seminar's September meeting—just a month before the report was issued, notes Gary—Marshall reported that the foundation's projects would engage "the threefold task of maintaining civilian morale at home, of maintaining good relations with friendly countries, and of waging propaganda warfare with countries hostile to us."[55]

Even as the report was distributed to a number of scholars, university presidents, foundation officers, publishers, and government officials,[56] Marshall and Lasswell were approaching government officials and, in Gary's words, "quietly made it known that foundation monies might be available to facilitate government-needed communication research."[57] From early 1940 until the U.S. entry into the war in December 1941, the foundation served, in essence, as an unofficial arm of the state when the Roosevelt administration—hampered by a public culture still wary of propaganda, and a somewhat isolationist Congress—could not feasibly do so itself. Marshall was quite candid about this in his proposals to the Rockefeller trustees:

> Whether or not this is something for the foundation to consider, I do not know. . . But the early neglect of this type of study [by others] may mean that it is the only agency as yet ready to recognize its importance and to provide the necessary funds. . . for the type of work which later may be needed in national defense.[58]

Fellow Rockefeller officer Stacey May, who was at the time also working with the Office of Emergency Management, wrote to Marshall to warn him that the "last war left the country suspicious of propaganda" and that, as a result, the government would be "slow to develop 'morale' activities for fear of being accused of propagandizing."[59]

Gary documents that, in his response, Marshall agreed and observed that even "communications research" was plagued by propaganda fears. Despite the "growing recognition of the need for such research," he continued, any Roosevelt-led efforts "would not be looked on favorably by Congress."[60] By the end of 1940, the foundation had set up and funded an elaborate bundle of propaganda-related projects; even those research initiatives, such as the ORR, that were originally conceived with other purposes were, by this time, brought into the propaganda fold. By 1940, Rockefeller-backed projects included Cantril's Princeton Public Opinion Research Project (which the foundation had funded after Cantril split with Lazarsfeld); the Princeton Shortwave Listening Center; the Graduate Library Reading Project at Chicago; the Film Library of the Museum of Modern Art (which included Siegfried Kracauer's studies of Nazi film propaganda); the Library of Congress Radio Project; the Totalitarian Communications Project at the New School; and Lasswell's content analysis operation at the Library of Congress.[61]

As Gary establishes, the Communications Seminar set the agenda for, and helped to mobilize, the extraordinary Rockefeller campaign to build up a wartime propaganda apparatus when the government itself could not. The Seminar's intellectual agenda for "communications research"—a term, as Sproule shows, that was self-consciously selected as a fresh alternative to the Progressive "propaganda analysis" label—was, in part, shaped by the world crisis and the felt need to understand, and master, persuasion technique. Many of the scholars' preferences for particular, and often quantitative, methods predated the Seminar. Nonetheless, the selection of so many figures central to public opinion research, along with the consensus building of the Seminar process itself, surely helped to establish quantitative techniques at the center of the wartime and postwar mass communication research agenda.

WORLD WAR II AND THE EARLY COLD WAR:
STATE-FUNDED "PSYCHOLOGICAL WARFARE"

Timothy Glander and Christopher Simpson pick up where Gary, Buxton, and Sproule leave off: the massive wartime propaganda effort. Based on extensive archival research, Glander and Simpson show that the extraordinary social scientific mobilization for "psychological warfare" work fostered social networks and an intellectual framework that shaped the communication field long after the Axis powers were vanquished. Their argument is that the scholars (such as Lazarsfeld, Schramm, Lasswell, and Daniel Lerner) and the questions (concerning effective propaganda design) from the war period were, in essence, redeployed in the early cold war. Both scholars uncover an extensive set of once-classified or long-forgotten studies, funded by the military, State Department, and CIA (with some foundation collusion) throughout the 1950s and into the 1960s, preoccupied with the task of making propaganda work.

Simpson's 1994 *Science of Coercion* is the more exhaustively researched effort. Simpson, an investigative journalist who has produced a number of blistering exposes in other areas, does not conceal his leftist political commitments.[62] Despite its polemical tone, Simpson's book convincingly shows that the traditional "limited effects" storyline is woefully inadequate to explain postwar communication research. Indeed, he suggests (though does not develop) the point that, especially after the mid-1950s when the campaign for third world hearts and minds heated up, prominent published research was based on secret propaganda work that was repackaged as disinterested science. Glander, an education scholar, covers much of the same territory as Simpson in his 2000 *Origins of Mass Communications Research during the American Cold War,* based on a 1988 dissertation.[63] Glander's work is useful mainly as a supplement to Simpson's, as it includes some new detail and archival sources[64] but in other respects confirms the *Science of Coercion* narrative.

Both scholars stress the crucial importance of social scientists' wartime service. Hundreds of social scientists temporarily left their academic posts to take up direct employment or consultancies for dozens of government and military agencies—an always-evolving acronymic tangle of programs and departments including, most prominently, the Army's Research Branch, the Office of Strategic Services (precursor to the CIA), the Office of Wartime Information, and the Library of Congress, but also the Departments of Justice and of Agriculture, the FCC, and many others. Perhaps more importantly, the employment overlap of constantly shuffled scholars produced networks of contacts, friendships, and acquaintances that proved, after the war, to be of extraordinary importance to many disciplines and to various lines of scholarship—including, as it turned out, mass communication research itself.

Much of that wartime social science was concerned with the design and testing of propaganda—"psychological warfare," as the bundle of techniques and theory came to be known.[65] Simpson and Glander show that, when the cold war heated up in the late 1940s, the federal government in effect reconstituted its World War II propaganda infrastructure. Scholars who had been working in Washington were, by the early 1950s, spread about at research institutes modeled on Lazarsfeld's BASR. Federal money—from the military, CIA, and State Department, often in close coordination with foundations such as Carnegie and Ford—poured into these university-based research institutes, as Simpson meticulously documents.[66] Throughout most of the 1950s, and with no public acknowledgment, government funds made up more than three-quarters of the annual budget at Lazarsfeld's Bureau, Cantril's Institute for International Social Research at Princeton, Ithiel de Sola Pool's Center for International Studies at MIT, and similar research shops.[67] Simpson concludes that these Bureau-style institutes grew up as "de facto adjuncts of government psychological warfare programs."[68]

The detailed findings of Simpson and Glander are so startling in part because they drastically contradict the field's "limited effects" self-narration—the claim that postwar media research had discovered that mass media influence is happily negligible. Even while "limited effects"-style conclusions were published, in *Personal Influence* for example, research outfits like Lazarsfeld and Katz's Bureau were under federal contract to design effective propaganda campaigns overseas.[69] Though critics of the "dominant paradigm" like Gitlin had stressed the influence of funders, the critics' indictment had pointed to media industry patrons who, according to the argument, were let off the hook by the "limited effects" conclusion. Simpson and Glander draw altogether different conclusions: The Bureau was hardly concerned to show that media influence is limited, since it was in the business of making persuasion work for its commercial and government clients.

Much of the federally funded research, Simpson and Glander show, was directed at third world populations deemed susceptible to Soviet influence. Rohan Samarajiva, a respected development communication scholar and the final "new historian" I identify here, has exposed a significant example of the wider pattern described by Simpson and Glander. Samarajiva, in a brilliant though little-noticed 1987 paper, revisits Daniel Lerner's classic, *The Passing of Traditional Society: Modernizing the Middle East* (1958). In the paper—aptly titled "The Murky Beginnings of the Communication and Development Field"—Samarajiva reveals that the book was spun-off from a sprawling and largely secret audience research project funded by the Voice of America.[70] The project, awarded to Lazarsfeld's Bureau in 1949, was explicitly tasked with identifying target audiences for U.S.

propaganda in the Middle East.[71] During World War II, Lerner had worked with Edward Shils and Morris Janowitz in the Psychological Warfare Division of Eisenhower's Allied command, and after the war wrote a dissertation (published as *Sykewar* in 1949) on the anti-Nazi propaganda effort.[72] Lerner (and a number of other Bureau figures) helped oversee the field interviews in 1950 and 1951—nearly 2,000 were conducted across the Middle East.[73] In *Passing*, Lerner acknowledges that the book is based on Bureau surveys, but says nothing about government funding or the study's original purpose.[74] Indeed, Lerner claims he is motivated by the "historic shift. . . of modernist inspiration from the discreet discourse of a few . . . to the broadcast exhortations among the multitudes."[75] To Samarajiva, Lerner's failure to disclose the study's original context amounts to "willful suppression," a "lie by omission"—and helps to demonstrate how "modernization" was largely a euphemism for ongoing cold war psychological warfare.[76]

THE NEW HISTORY: AN ASSESSMENT

The new history, as a body of work, presents an astonishing indictment of the field's intellectual progenitors and their whitewashed remembrances. One inescapable conclusion is that the field's remembered history—of four founders and the reassuring "limited effects" findings—obscures a major thrust of postwar mass communication research: "psychological warfare" studies on behalf of, and funded by, various government agencies for use in overseas and domestic cold war propaganda campaigns.

Each of the new histories takes into account the array of external pressures—intellectual and otherwise—that have helped shape the would-be discipline. Most of the preexisting historiography, in contrast, has been resolutely internalist, neglectful even of intellectual influences from outside the field. The bulk of that earlier history is concerned with legitimating the field from within and without. Significantly, the new history revises even the *revisionist* history (of Gitlin and others) that had, as we have seen, accepted core elements of the mainstream story.

The new history is distinguished, too, by its rigor and archival burrowing, and here again the contrast to a long line of footnote-less digests is striking. To varying degrees, the new history is acquainted with the rich methodological reflection in the history and sociology of science fields. And, perhaps more importantly, the new history by and large embraces a laudable explanatory eclecticism—a refusal to settle on a single mode of analysis. There is simply too much complexity and diversity in the field's past for any unitary scheme to bear much explanatory burden—without, at least, inflicting major violence on the empirical reality that it purports to explain. The new history, for the most part, submits to a case-by-case explanatory agnosticism that lets the empirical evidence "assert" itself first.

These features of the new history, to borrow Alun Jones' 1983 description, "bear a suspicious resemblance to what most professional historians would identify as simply 'good history.'"[77] Even so, the six historians' work has its limitations—most notably in scope—and we would do well to consider their research as a foundation on which to build.

The new history, for example, does not adequately place the study of communication in the context of "public opinion research," the interdisciplinary social science field that grew up after 1936 around polling methods and emerged, after the wartime propaganda effort, at the center of postwar empirical social science. From 1936 until the "communication" field had substantially migrated to journalism schools by the early 1960s, public opinion (or survey) research was, indeed, hard to distinguish from "communication" study.[78] The new history also neglects the fascinating relationship between 1950s communication research and the public intellectual debates over "mass culture" then raging. Most significantly, the synthetic account that emerges from the bundle of histories ends rather abruptly, in the early 1960s—just as the slow march through journalism schools had picked up pace. We remain almost wholly ignorant of the field's history as an institutionalized "discipline," and here the new history provides little relief.

More generally, the new history is not informed well enough by the substantial and growing body of historical research on postwar social science.[79] Historians of communication research should be immersed in this literature, if only because the field, especially before the migration to journalism schools, was nothing but a loose assemblage of sociologists, psychologists, and political scientists. Most of the other social sciences have subdisciplines devoted to their disciplinary histories, and benefit from the attendant cross-pollination and organizational momentum. The new history of communication research, as with the rest of the field's historiography, does not seem to be self-conscious of itself as a community of collaborating scholars. Few of the historians cite one another, and in many instances seem unaware of the others' work. The infrastructure of scholarship—conferences, journals, and associations, and the linked intangibles of friendships and a sense of common knowledge goals—these are missing.

There are specific, substantive problems too. Gary, for instance, is too taken with the quite genuine dilemmas of interwar liberalism, and as a result downplays the crucial, and interwoven, roles of funding and opportunism. Simpson and Glander err in the opposite direction, in their overcommitment to an otherwise laudable resource-based sociology of knowledge. One of the drawbacks of such an approach is that the complex and distinct motives of key researchers get neglected. It is important, for example, to distinguish between zealous cold warriors like Wilbur Schramm or Daniel Lerner and apolitical funding opportunists like Lazarsfeld.

It's also true that the new historians—especially Simpson, Glander, and Sproule—could make a more strenuous effort to narrate the field's past in its own terms, rather than through present concerns. Simpson's muckraking zeal to uncover the field's original sin, for example, leads him to underplay the elective affinity between genuinely held cold war liberalism and the goals of the national security state. Here George Stocking's 1965 call for an "enlightened presentism," in which a rigorous effort to understand the past "for its own sake" is tempered by acknowledgment of the attempt's limits, should be our guide.[80]

CONCLUSION

Kurt Danziger, the historian of psychology, described the state of the subfield before a wave of revisionist historiography in the 1970s and 1980s: "Historical scholarship," he wrote, "came a distant second to the primary function of the field which was pedagogical, imparting an appropriate group image to aspirant members of the discipline."[81] Danziger's description could readily apply to communication studies and its remembered history today, were it not for the recent contributions of what I have here called the "new history."

Still, the question remains: why did this body of work emerge so "late" relative to the other social sciences? How is it that, as early as 1966, Stocking could speak of an "upsurge" of interest in the history of anthropology—when, decades later, no such surge had materialized within communication research?[82]

In conclusion, I want to propose a possible answer. In a field with little in common save a label, selective memory and forgetting play outsized roles in holding the discipline together. John Peel once observed that there is an inverse correlation between our ability to narrate the past faithfully and the functions that a remembered "past" performs for a community.[83] Communication research, as a field, badly needs the glue of tradition, however invented.

This is true because of the field's peculiar (and intellectually retarding) institutionalization—in journalism schools, speech departments, and other sites scattered across the university.[84] Faculty who work under the "communication" label are normally expected to produce scholarship and, at the same time, impart career skills to industry-bound students. In practice, this means polarized departments or else schizophrenic faculty. "The fact that a single individual can teach courses in, say, magazine editing and research techniques in social psychology," observed Jeremy Tunstall back in 1983, "is a tribute to human adaptability, not to a well-conceived academic discipline."[85]

For all its incoherence as an institutionalized discipline, communication is endowed with abundant resources, including an enormous supply of undergraduate would-be celebrities. But because of its vocational taint—and its messy and recently formed institutional trappings—the field has from the beginning endured a deficit in legitimacy. Even internal to the field, there are very few shared conceptual underpinnings. In short, the field has (in Andrew Abbott's terms) a social structure without much cultural coherence.[86]

Much rests, then, on the field's self-narration of its past. Whiggishness and intellectual continuity are crucial, as is a kind of forgetting—notably, of the field's checkered institutional roots.[87] The rigorous scrutiny of communication's past might fray the discipline's fragile bonds. Recall Stephen Brush's famous question, whether the history of science should be "rated X" for its potential to undermine students' faith in science.[88] Perhaps the new history of communication research took so long to emerge—and even now registers so weakly in the field's consciousness—because the discipline has needed all the faith it can muster.

NOTES

1. "Approaches to the Historical Development," 41.
2. The reference is to the 1983 special issue of the *Journal of Communication*, in which more than two dozen scholars challenged (or, less frequently, defended) the mainstream "effects tradition" of the postwar field (see "Ferment in the Field").
3. The best analysis of this institutionalization remains John Durham Peters's "Institutional Sources of Intellectual Poverty in Communication Research." But the field's institutional history remains strikingly understudied (see Introduction, this volume). There are bits and pieces of such a history in various accounts, especially Delia, "Communication Research: A History," 73–84; Chaffee and Rogers, "The Establishment of Communication Study in America"; Weaver, "Journalism and Mass Communication Research"; Marjorie Fish's underappreciated dissertation ("A Study of Mass Communication Research," 54–70); Cartier, "Wilbur Schramm and the Beginnings of American Communication Theory," 243–76; King, "A History of the Department"; Katzen, *Mass Communication*, 19–55; and Sproule, this volume.
4. This mutual neglect was on vivid display in 1994, when two book-length histories (Rogers, *A History of Communication Study* and Cohen, *The History of Speech Communication*) were published, rooted in the journalism- and speech-derived traditions, respectively. As Robert Craig observed, the books have almost no overlap (review, 181). My focus is on the history remembered by the mass communication tradition.
5. Katz and Lazarsfeld do not use "hypodermic needle" or "magic bullet" in *Personal Influence*, but these became the standard shorthands for the "limited effects" narrative. Katz did first employ the "hypodermic" metaphor, in this context, in an unpublished 1953 report (see Simonson, Introduction, 16–17). On the evolution of the "hypodermic" label, see Lubken, this volume.
6. On the formation of this limited effects storyline, see Pooley, "Fifteen Pages"; and, in more detail, Pooley, "An Accident of Memory." See also Pietilä, "Perspectives on Our Past," 347–50.

7. Schramm, who before World War II was a professor of English at the University of Iowa (where he helped found the Iowa Writers' Workshop), volunteered for the war propaganda effort in December 1941. After he left government in late 1943—excited about the possibilities for communication as a new field—he transformed Iowa's journalism school into a school of "Journalism and Mass Communication" complete with a PhD program, leading other Midwestern universities (including Minnesota and Wisconsin) to follow suit. Schramm moved to the University of Illinois in 1948 and founded the first of three institutes of communication research (modeled after Lazarsfeld's Bureau). This story has been told many times, usually in a celebratory fashion. See, for example, Chaffee and others, "The Contributions of Wilbur Schramm"; McAnany, "Wilbur Schramm, 1907–1987"; Cartier, "Wilbur Schramm and the Beginnings of American Communication Theory"; Keever, "Wilbur Schramm"; and Chaffee and Rogers, "Wilbur Schramm, the Founder."

8. "Communication Research in the United States," 2. The four were first designated as distinct lineages by Bernard Berelson in 1958 and 1959 ("Present State" and "State of Communication Research").

9. "Communication Research in the United States," 2.

10. Ibid., 5.

11. Ibid.

12. "The Beginnings of Communication Research"; "The Unique Perspective of Communication"; "The Beginnings of Communication Study"; and (posthumously) *The Beginnings of Communication Study*.

13. I am indebted to Veikko Pietilä's excellent essay, which makes this point convincingly ("Perspectives on Our Past," 150–51).

14. Gitlin's reliance on commercial funding simply cannot perform the heavy lifting that he asks it to do—despite the fact that Lazarsfeld did indeed package some of his findings in a media-friendly way, especially if the executives were the intended audience. And certain Bureau-linked figures, most prominently Frank Stanton of CBS and Joseph Klapper, who by the late 1950s had also joined CBS, were indeed carrying the industry's water in a more-or-less shameless way. But Lazarsfeld, with his genuine scientific interests and aspirations, was much more complicated. (See Pooley, "An Accident of Memory," 179–299.) As Christopher Simpson and Timothy Glander show, moreover, government propaganda funding during the war and especially in the 1950s was a more important source of funds (see discussion, below).

15. "Media Sociology: The Dominant Paradigm," 207.

16. As Pietilä observes, critical scholars did not draft a new history as much as judge the standard history "in an entirely different way" ("Perspectives on Our Past," 151). Pietilä: "one gets the impression that the New Left version is not motivated by an ardent interest in the past as much as creating a weapon in the struggle for hegemony in the field during the ferment of the late seventies and early eighties" (Ibid.).

17. The key diffusion figure here was James Halloran of the University of Leicester, whose 1964 *Effects of Mass Communication* and other writings in the late 1960s and early 1970s framed the American sociology of media for the two major traditions of 1970s British media research, political economy and cultural studies.

18. See, for example, Lang, "The Critical Functions of Empirical Communication Research"; and Lang and Lang, "The 'New' Rhetoric of Mass Communication Research." Lang and Lang do assert, in these works and elsewhere, that the "magic bullet" contrast is largely a straw man, but do not challenge the "limited effects" emplotting. Rowland's *The Politics of TV Violence* is a rich and detailed study of the field's entanglements in public policy debates over TV violence, but

the book also largely accepts the "limited effects" self-description. Morrison's dissertation ("Paul Lazarsfeld") and follow-up work ("The Beginnings of Modern Mass Communication Research") reproduces (with terrific, interview-based detail, however) the *Personal Influence* storyline. (On Morrison's more recent work, see n. 19.) Czitrom's treatment ("The Rise of Empirical Media Study"), like the Langs', asserts that the putative "powerful effects" contrast is a straw man, but otherwise accepts the "limited effects" narrative. Delia's exhaustive "Communication Research: A History," likewise, accepts the standard "limited effects" self-characterization.

19. I exclude here some recent work that, by the criteria of rigor and sophistication alone, would be included, but that does not substantially challenge the field's received history. In this excluded-but-worthy category, recent work by David Morrison (e.g., "Late Arrival," "Influences Influencing"), Peter Simonson (e.g., Introduction, "Serendipity"), and Karin Wahl-Jorgensen (e.g., "Rebellion and Ritual," "How Not to Found a Field") stands out.

20. For a history of the ORR that draws on Buxton, Sproule, and Gary, see Pooley, "An Accident of Memory," 179–299.

21. *Talcott Parsons and the Capitalist Nation-State.*

22. See especially "The Political Economy of Communications Research" and "From Radio Research to Communications Intelligence." "Reaching Human Minds" and "John Marshall and the Humanities" add some more detail. Much of Buxton's more recent work has focused on excavating the thought of Canadian economist Harold A. Innis (including "The 'Values' Discussion Group").

23. For an example, see "The Emergence of Communications Study."

24. *The Nervous Liberals.*

25. "Communication Research, the Rockefeller Foundation, and Mobilization for the War on Words."

26. See especially "Propaganda Studies in American Social Science"; "Progressive Critics and the Magic Bullet Myth"; "Propaganda and American Ideological Critique"; and *Propaganda and Democracy.*

27. "Political Economy of Communications Research," 154–56.

28. Ibid., 154–55.

29. Ibid., 155–56.

30. "In effect, the Rockefeller Foundation assumed a task that neither broadcasters, educators, nor state officials were willing or able to undertake" (Ibid., 153).

31. It is only a slight exaggeration that, as Buxton argues, Marshall "almost single-handedly gave coherence and direction to the assorted Rockefeller projects related to the relatively new media of mass communication" (Ibid., 156). His crucial contributions were not so much intellectual but financial and organizational. As Gary observes, his interests in radio were "largely derivative and synthetic, and not especially original. His importance should be measured by his role as an administrative catalyst and agent for scholars, and not for the questions he asked or the problems he framed" ("Communication Research, the Rockefeller Foundation," 130.)

32. Buxton, "Political Economy of Communications Research," 158.

33. Buxton: "While the Act set the framework for the incorporation of educational interests into the commercial broadcasting system, it did not provide the resources, programs, and expertise through which this reconciliation between educators and broadcasters could take place . . . the role of charting the path of cooperation between educational and broadcasting interests fell to the Humanities Program of the Rockefeller Foundation" (Ibid., 153).

34. Ibid., 160.

35. Marshall, "Reminiscences."

36. "Political Economy of Communications Research," 161–64.
37. Ibid., 160–61.
38. Ibid., 164. From the Cantril and Stanton proposal: "If radio in the United States is to serve the best interest of the people, it is essential that an objective analysis be made of what these interests are and how the unique psychological and social characteristics of radio may be devoted to them" (164).
39. Ibid., 167.
40. Ibid.
41. Ibid.; and Gary, "Communication Research, the Rockefeller Foundation," 132.
42. Oral history interview, quoted in Pasanella, *The Mind Traveller*, 13.
43. Ibid., 12.
44. Gary: "With war breaking out in Europe, Rockefeller officers and the founding fathers of communication research were galvanized by the recognition that the Roosevelt Administration, hamstrung politically, could not adequately prepare for war on the propaganda front. Isolationist sentiment and bad memories from World War I limited the administration's ability to influence domestic public opinion or control foreign and domestic antidemocratic propaganda. The Rockefeller Foundation, whose university-, museum-, and library-based projects had more room to experiment with potentially controversial activities, took up the slack. With Marshall and the Foundation providing funding and serving midwife roles, Rockefeller-funded research laid the groundwork for a wide range of national security projects that were eventually absorbed by the state" ("Communication Research, the Rockefeller Foundation," 125).
45. See Sproule, "Propaganda Studies in American Social Science."
46. Gary's broader argument, laid out in most detail in his 1999 book *The Nervous Liberals*, is framed in terms of two major debates among post–World War I liberals. He describes, in impressive detail, the debate, from the early 1920s on, between chastened realists like Walter Lippmann and progressive populists as to the competence of the public in terms of democratic theory and practice. Gary argues that, with this debate in the background, a second major conflict came to the fore with the rise of fascism, World War II, and the possible U.S. entry: a debate that pitted traditional liberal concerns for civil liberties against emergency-context national security concerns. Many liberals, even those who had in the 1920s opposed Lippmann's view, came to help in the building of what Gary rather generously calls a "propaganda prophylaxis"—a set of state-driven defenses against fascist propaganda that involved propping up U.S. domestic morale and countering fascist propaganda at home and abroad. Gary makes it quite clear that this "propaganda prophylaxis" and the wartime service of communication scholars was an honorable, good faith effort—retroactively justifiable given the uniquely "just war" context. He allows, though, for a kind of unintended consequence of well-intentioned action: this good faith, emergency effort became routinized, through inertia and the subsequent cold war context, into the national security state, whose propaganda activities are less defensible.
47. See "Communication Research, the Rockefeller Foundation," 131, for a summary of the proposal.
48. Quoted in Ibid., 132.
49. The Seminar's nonfoundation participants were Lazarsfeld; Harold Lasswell; Robert Lynd; Hadley Cantril; Geoffrey Gorer, an Oxford-trained anthropologist; Lyman Bryson, an adult education specialist; Donald Slesinger, former dean of the Social Sciences at Chicago and director of the Rockefeller-funded American Film Center; I.A. Richards, the prominent Canadian literary theorist; Douglas Waples of the University of Chicago's library school (and mentor to Bernard Berelson, who began his academic career there); Charles Siepmann, a communication analysis

for the BBC; and Lloyd Free, the once and future Cantril collaborator who would, in 1940, take over the editorship of the *Public Opinion Quarterly* and after the war participate centrally in the cold war propaganda efforts (Ibid., 133).

50. "Propaganda Studies in American Social Science," 75.
51. As Gary observes: "Normally attributed solely to Lasswell, the paradigm was the product of months of paper exchanges, seminars, and oral and written dialogue, among diverse members" ("Communication Research, the Rockefeller Foundation," 138.)
52. Quoted in Ibid., 139.
53. Ibid., 140.
54. Ibid., 141.
55. Quoted in Ibid.
56. Including, as Gary reports, Robert Hutchins, Louis Wirth, Henry Luce, Talcott Parsons, William O. Douglas, and Archibald MacLeish (Ibid., 142).
57. Ibid.
58. Quoted in Ibid., 143.
59. Quoted in Ibid.
60. Quoted in Ibid.
61. Ibid., 125.
62. See, for example, *War Crimes of the Deutsche Bank* and *The Splendid Blond Beast*.
63. "The Battle for the Minds of Men." See also Glander, "Wilbur Schramm."
64. Glander establishes, for example, that Schramm was almost certainly on the CIA payroll and the secret informant that nearly scuttled Dallas Smythe's appointment at the University of Illinois in 1948 (170–72).
65. The best overview of social scientists' government propaganda service is Converse, *Survey Research*, 162–228.
66. *Science of Coercion*, 4, chaps. 5–6.
67. Ibid., 4.
68. Ibid.
69. This contrast between a *frontstage* "limited effects" finding and a *backstage* search for workable propaganda strategy is suggested, but undeveloped, by Simpson and Glander.
70. "Murky Beginnings," 6. See also Samarajiva, "Tainted Origins of Development Communication."
71. "Murky Beginnings," 6–8.
72. Samarajiva quotes the final paragraph of *Sykewar*: "In its 'cold war' with the Soviet Union... the United States is offering mainly dollars... to produce more 'good things of life.' ... Should it turn out that ... the 'good things' we offer are not adequate competition against the 'better world' offered by the Soviets, we shall need some new policy decisions... Here we shall need to consult the intelligence specialists (the social scientist) and the communication specialist (the propagandist)—rather than, or in addition to, the diplomat, the economist, and the soldier" (6–7).
73. Ibid., 7.
74. Ibid.
75. Quoted in Ibid., 7–8. Adds Samarajiva: "The investigation that led to this paper was sparked by the difficulties experienced by this writer in attempting to evaluate *Traditional Society* as part of a graduate course. The natural question as to what the original research questions, were, proved difficult to answer" (14).
76. Ibid., 3, 14.
77. "The New History of Sociology," 458.

78. See Pooley, "An Accident of Memory," 216–30. Converse's *Survey Research* is an excellent overview.
79. The literature is far too broad to cite, but see Crowther-Heyck, "Patrons of the Revolution," 421–24, for an excellent review.
80. Stocking, "On the Limits of 'Presentism,'" 8–11.
81. "Concluding Comments," 208.
82. "The History of Anthropology," 281.
83. Peel, *Herbert Spencer*, cited in Jones, "New History," 456.
84. Peters ("Institutional Sources") makes this case convincingly. As Robert Craig has noted, "The field or discipline of communication as we presently know it has sprung from no single source and has no coherence" (review, 178).
85. "The Trouble with U.S. Communication Research," 93.
86. Abbott, *Chaos of Disciplines*, 122. Abbott's distinction mirrors Richard Whitley's contrast between "social" and "cognitive" institutionalization ("Cognitive and Social Institutionalization").
87. Here the parallel with national identity, in Ernst Renan's famous stress on the importance of forgetting, is striking ("What is a Nation?").
88. "Should the History of Science be Rated X?"

WORKS CITED

Abbott, Andrew D. *Chaos of Disciplines*. Chicago: University of Chicago Press, 2001.
Bannister, Robert C. *Sociology and Scientism: The American Quest for Objectivity, 1880–1940*. Chapel Hill: University of North Carolina Press, 1987.
Berelson, Bernard. "The Present State of Communication Research." *Public Opinion Quarterly* 22, no. 2 (1958): 178.
———. "The State of Communication Research." *Public Opinion Quarterly* 23, no. 1 (1959): 1–5.
Brown, R.L. "Approaches to the Historical Development of Mass Media Studies." In *Media Sociology: A Reader*, edited by Jeremy Tunstall, 41–57. Urbana: University of Illinois Press, 1970.
Brush, Stephen. "Should the History of Science be Rated X?" *Science* 183 (1974): 1164–72.
Buxton, William. "The Emergence of Communications Study—Psychological Warfare or Scientific Thoroughfare?" *Canadian Journal of Communication* 21, no. 4 (1996). http://www.cjc-online.ca/viewarticle.php?id=384.
———. "From Radio Research to Communications Intelligence: Rockefeller Philanthropy, Communications Specialists, and the American Intelligence Community." In *The Political Influence of Ideas: Policy Communities and the Social Sciences*, edited by A.G Gagnon and Stephen Brooks, 187–209. Westport, CT: Greenwood, 1994.
———. "John Marshall and the Humanities in Europe: Shifting Patterns of Rockefeller Support." *Minerva* 41, no. 2 (2003): 133–53.
———. "The Political Economy of Communications Research." In *Information and Communication in Economics*, edited by Robert E. Babe, 147–75. Boston: Kluwer Academic Publishers, 1994.
———. "Reaching Human Minds: Rockefeller Philanthropy and Communications, 1935–1939." In *The Development of the Social Sciences in the United States and Canada: The Role of Philanthropy Policy Issues in Education*, edited by Theresa R. Richardson and Donald Fisher, 177–92. Stamford, CT: Ablex, 1999.
———. *Talcott Parsons and the Capitalist Nation-State: Political Sociology as a Strategic Vocation*. Toronto: University of Toronto Press, 1985.

———. "The 'Values' Discussion Group at the University of Toronto, February–May 1949." *Canadian Journal of Communication* 29, no. 2 (2004). http://www.cjc-online.ca/viewarticle. php?id=877.

Cartier, Jacqueline Marie. "Wilbur Schramm and the Beginnings of American Communication Theory: A History of Ideas." PhD diss., University of Iowa, 1988.

Chaffee, Steven H., G.C. Chu, Jack Lyle, and W. Danielson. "The Contributions of Wilbur Schramm to Mass Communication Research." *Journalism Monographs* 36 (1974).

Chaffee, Steven H., and Everett M. Rogers. "The Establishment of Communication Study in America." In *The Beginnings of Communication Study in America: A Personal Memoir*, edited by Steven H. Chaffee and Everett M. Rogers, 125–80. Thousand Oaks, CA: Sage, 1997.

———. "Wilbur Schramm, the Founder." In *The Beginnings of Communication Study in America: A Personal Memoir*, edited by Steven H. Chaffee and Everett M. Rogers, 126–76. Thousand Oaks, CA: Sage, 1997.

Cohen, Herman. *The History of Speech Communication: The Emergence of a Discipline, 1914–1945.* Annandale, VA: Speech Communication Association, 1994.

Converse, Jean M. *Survey Research in the United States: Roots and Emergence, 1890–1960.* Berkeley: University of California Press, 1987.

Craig, Robert T. Review of a *History of Communication Study: A Biographical Approach*, by Everett M. Rogers, and the *History of Speech Communication: The Emergence of a Discipline 1914–1945*, by Herbert Cohen. *Communication Theory* 5 (1995): 178–84.

Crowther-Heyck, Hunter. "Patrons of the Revolution: Ideals and Institutions in Postwar Behavioral Science." *Isis* 97 (2006): 420–46.

Czitrom, Daniel. "The Rise of Empirical Media Study: Communications Research as Behavioral Science, 1930–1960." In *Media and the American Mind*, 122–46. Chapel Hill: University of North Carolina Press, 1982.

Danziger, Kurt. "Concluding Comments." In *Rediscovering the History of Psychology: Essays Inspired By the Work of Kurt Danziger*, edited by Adrian C. Brock, Johann Louw, and Willem van Hoorn, 207–31. New York: Kluwer Academic/Plenum Publishers, 2004.

Delia, Jesse G. "Communication Research: A History." In *Handbook of Communication Science*, edited by Charles R. Berger; Steven H. Chaffee; 20–98. Newbury Park, CA: Sage , 1987.

Fish, Marjorie Jane. "A Study of Mass Communication Research and Scholarship." PhD diss., University of Texas, 1984.

Gary, Brett. "Communication Research, the Rockefeller Foundation, and Mobilization for the War on Words." *Journal of Communication* 46, no. 3 (1996): 124–47.

———. *The Nervous Liberals: Propaganda Anxieties From World War I to the Cold War.* New York: Columbia University Press, 1999.

Gerbner, George, and Marsha Siefert, eds. "Ferment in the Field [Special Issue]." *Journal of Communication* 33, no. 3 (1983).

Gitlin, Todd. "Media Sociology: The Dominant Paradigm." *Theory and Society* 6 (1978): 205–53.

Glander, Timothy. "The Battle for the Minds of Men: Wilbur Schramm at the University of Illinois, 1947–1953." PhD diss., University of Illinois, 1988.

———. *Origins of Mass Communications Research during the American Cold War: Educational Effects and Contemporary Implications.* Mahwah, NJ: Lawrence Erlbaum, 2000.

———. "Wilbur Schramm and the Founding of Communication Studies." *Educational Theory* 46, no. 3 (1996): 373–91.

Halloran, James D. *The Effects of Mass Communication.* Leicester, UK: Leicester University Press, 1964.

Jones, Robert Alun. "The New History of Sociology." *Annual Review of Sociology* 9 (1983): 447–69.

Katz, Elihu, and Paul F. Lazarsfeld. *Personal Influence: The Part Played By People in the Flow of Mass Communications.* Glencoe, IL: Free Press, 1955.

Katzen, May. *Mass Communication: Teaching and Studies at Universities.* Paris, France: UNESCO Press, 1975.

Keever, Beverly Ann. "Wilbur Schramm: On Windwagons and Sky Busters: Final Regrets of a Mass Communication Pioneer." *Mass Communication Review* 1 (1991): 3–26.

King, Larry Jene. "A History of the Department of Communication at the University of Oklahoma: A Case Study in the History of the Discipline." PhD diss., University of Oklahoma, 1990.

Lang, Kurt. "The Critical Functions of Empirical Communication Research." In *Mass Communication Review Yearbook (1),* edited by G.C. Wilhoit and Harold de Bock, 45–58. Beverly Hills, CA: Sage, 1980.

Lang, Kurt, and Gladys E. Lang. "The 'New' Rhetoric of Mass Communication Research: A Longer View." *Journal of Communication* 33, no. 3 (1983): 128–40.

Lerner, Daniel. *The Passing of Traditional Society: Modernizing the Middle East.* Glencoe, IL: Free Press, 1958.

Lerner, Daniel. *Sykewar: Psychological Warfare against Germany, D-Day to VE-Day.* New York: G.W.Stewart, 1949.

Marshall, John. "Reminiscences of John Marshall and Charlotte T. Marshall." 1974, transcript and tape, Oral History Research Office, Rare Book & Manuscript Library, Columbia University, New York.

McAnany, Emile G. "Wilbur Schramm, 1907–1987: Roots of the Past, Seeds of the Present." *Journal of Communication* 38, no. 4 (1988): 109–22.

Morrison, David. "The Beginnings of Modern Mass Communication Research." *European Journal of Sociology* 19 (1978): 347–59.

———. "The Influences Influencing *Personal Influence:* Scholarship and Entrepreneurship." In "Politics, Social Networks, and the History of Mass Communications Research: Rereading *Personal Influence,*" edited by Peter Simonson, special issue. *Annals of the American Academy of Political and Social Sciences* 608 (2006): 51–75.

———. "The Late Arrival of Television Research: A Case Study in the Production of Knowledge." In "Media Power, Professionals, and Policies," edited by Howard Tumber. New York: Routledge, 2000.

———. "Paul Lazarsfeld: The Biography of an Institutional Innovator." PhD diss., University of . Leiscester, 1976.

Pasanella, Ann K. *The Mind Traveller: A Guide to Paul F. Lazarsfeld's Communication Research Papers.* New York: Freedom Forum, 1994.

Peel, John. *Herbert Spencer: The Evolution of a Sociologist.* New York: Basic Books, 1971.

Peters, John Durham. "Institutional Sources of Intellectual Poverty in Communication Research." *Communication Research* 13, no. 4 (1986): 527–59.

Pietilä, Veikko. "Perspectives on Our Past: Charting the Histories of Mass Communication Studies." *Critical Studies in Mass Communication* 11 (1994): 346–61.

Platt, Jennifer. *A History of Sociological Research Methods in America.* Cambridge: Cambridge University Press, 1996.

Pooley, Jefferson. "An Accident of Memory: Edward Shils, Paul Lazarsfeld and the History of American Mass Communication Research." PhD diss., Columbia University, 2006.

———. "Fifteen Pages That Shook the Field: *Personal Influence,* Edward Shils, and the Remembered History of Mass Communication Research." In "Politics, Social Networks, and the History of Mass Communications Research: Rereading *Personal Influence,*" edited by Peter Simonson, special issue. *Annals of the American Academy of Political and Social Science* 608 (2006): 130–56.

Renan, Ernst. "What is a Nation?" edited by Homi K. Bhabha, 7–19. London: Routledge, 1990.

Rogers, Everett M. *A History of Communication Study: A Biographical Approach*. New York: Free Press, 1994.

Rowland, Jr., Willard D. *The Politics of TV Violence: Policy Uses of Communication Research*. Beverly Hills, CA: Sage, 1983.

Samarajiva, Rohan. "The Murky Beginnings of the Communication and Development Field: Voice of America and *The Passing of Traditional Society*." In *Rethinking Development Communication*, edited by Neville Jayaweera, Sarath Amunugama, and E. Tăi Ariyaratna, 3–19. Singapore: Asian Mass Communication Research and Information Centre, 1987.

———. "Tainted Origins of Development Communication." *Communicator [New Delhi]* (1985): 5–9.

Schramm, Wilbur. "The Beginnings of Communication Research in the United States." In *Communication Yearbook (4)*, edited by D. Nimmo, 73–82. New Brunswick, NJ: Transaction, 1980.

———. *The Beginnings of Communication Study in America: A Personal Memoir*, edited by Steven H. Chaffee and Everett M. Rogers. Thousand Oaks, CA: Sage, 1997.

———. "The Beginnings of Communication Study in the United States." In *The Media Revolution in America and in Western Europe*, edited by Everett M. Rogers and Fracis Balle, 200–11. Norwood, NJ: Ablex, 1985.

———. "Communication Research in the United States." In *The Science of Human Communication*, edited by Wilbur Schramm, 1–16. New York: Basic Books, 1963.

———. "The Unique Perspective of Communication: A Retrospective View." *Journal of Communication* 33 (1983): 6–17.

Simonson, Peter. Introduction to "Politics, Social Networks, and the History of Mass Communications Research: Rereading *Personal Influence*," edited by Peter Simonson, special issue. *Annals of the American Academy of Political and Social Science* 608 (2006): 6-24.

———. "The Serendipity of Merton's Communication Research." *International Journal of Public Opinion Research* 17, no. 3 (2005): 277–97.

Simpson, Christopher. *Science of Coercion: Communication Research and Psychological Warfare, 1945–1960*. New York: Oxford University Press, 1994.

———. *The Splendid Blond Beast: Money, Law, and Genocide in the Twentieth Century*. Monroe, ME: Common Courage Press, 1995.

———. *War Crimes of the Deutsche Bank and the Dresdner Bank: Office of Military Government (U.S.) Reports*. New York: Holmes & Meier, 2002.

Smith, Mark C. *Social Science in the Crucible: The American Debate over Objectivity and Purpose, 1918–1941*. Durham, NC: Duke University Press, 1994.

Sproule, J. Michael. "Progressive Critics and the Magic Bullet Myth." *Critical Studies in Mass Communication* 6 (1989): 225–46.

———. "Propaganda and American Ideological Critique." In *Communication Yearbook (14)*, edited by James A. Anderson, 211–39. Newbury Park, CA: Sage, 1991.

———. *Propaganda and Democracy: The American Experience of Media and Mass Persuasion*. Cambridge: Cambridge University Press, 1997.

———. "Propaganda Studies in American Social Science: The Rise and Fall of the Critical Paradigm." *Quarterly Journal of Speech* 73 (1987): 60–78.

Stocking, George W. "The History of Anthropology: Where, Whence, Whither?" *Journal for the History of the Behavioral Sciences* 2 (1966): 281–90.

———. "On the Limits of 'Presentism' and 'Historicism' in the Historiography of the Behavioral Sciences." In *Race, Culture, and Evolution: Essays in the History of Anthropology*, 1–12. Chicago: University of Chicago Press, 1965.

Tunstall, Jeremy. "The Trouble with U.S. Communication Research." *Journal of Communication* 33, no. 3 (1983): 92–95.

Wahl-Jorgensen, Karin. "Rebellion and Ritual in Disciplinary Histories of U.S. Mass Communication Study: Looking for 'the Reflexive Turn.'" *Mass Communication & Society* 3, no. 1 (2000): 87–115.

———. "How Not to Found a Field: New Evidence on the Origins of Mass Communication Research." *Journal of Communication* 54 (2004): 547–64.

Weaver, David H., and Richard G. Gray. "Journalism and Mass Communication Research in the United States." In *Mass Communication Review Yearbook (1)*, edited by G. Cleveland Wilhoit and Harold de Bock, 124–51. Beverly Hills, CA: Sage, 1980.

Whitley, Richard. "Cognitive and Social Institutionalization of Scientific Specialties and Research Areas." In *Social Processes of Scientific Development*, edited by Richard Whitley, 69–95. London: Routledge & Kegan Paul, 1974.

CHAPTER THREE

Walter Lippmann, Straw Man OF Communication Research

SUE CURRY JANSEN

> The unanimity of earlier historians, it seemed, had been the result of their borrowing from each other's narratives instead of returning to the original texts.
>
> —STEPHEN TOULMIN, *COSMOPOLIS*[1]

The neglect of history by the pioneers of mass communication scholarship has been extensively documented and critiqued.[2] This neglect imposed ideological blinders on researchers, stunted theoretical growth, and precluded development of a cumulative research tradition. Without a theory of society or adequate concepts of power, language, and culture, the field of communication, ironically contributed little to the so-called communication turn in scholarship that has energized epistemological debates in the humanities and social sciences in recent decades, and it is playing only a marginal role in current debates about propaganda and press freedom.

The field's indifference to history includes its own history. Yet, academic fields, like nation-states, require historical narratives: origin stories that define their boundaries legitimate their authority and ensure their futures.[3] As communication has lacked a coherent historical narrative, thin claims have filled the void and acquired resonance through repetition and reification. Over time, these claims have calcified into the "received wisdom" of the field. Consequently, those who would bring a new historical sensibility to communication do not encounter a blank slate. The terrain is littered with the debris of the legacy of neglect: partial truths, isolated facts, wishful thinking, caricatures, anecdotes, and inversions. In short, much of what now passes as history was never intended to carry that weight.

I want to thank Marsha Siefert, Jefferson Pooley, and Susan Ross for their encouragement and incisive readings of the manuscript.

In this chapter, I demonstrate how the neglect of history has contributed to the creation of a set of disciplinary-specific interpretive conventions—or "preferred readings"—of Walter Lippmann (1889–1974) that reduce him to a straw man and seriously misrepresent his work. These interpretative conventions tend to relieve critical historians of the responsibility of further direct engagement with—and struggle against—the work of a formidable thinker who posed deeply troubling questions about media and democracy, questions that those who are committed to advancing emancipatory communications cannot evade.

My goal is not to whitewash Lippmann's corpus, but merely to encourage an open, historically grounded, warts-and-all, reconsideration of a generative body of work that can still yield fresh insights. Before that can begin, however, current disciplinary-specific understandings of Lippmann require interrogation and challenge. That is the modest objective of this chapter: to clear away some of the litter and suggest alternative interpretive frames.

In advance, I must strongly emphasize that the range of my criticism is extremely narrow and tightly targeted. In challenging the preferred readings, I am only questioning the authors' interpretations of Lippmann, not their larger contributions to the field. In most cases, these contributions remain intact despite what I regard as disciplinarily skewed interpretations of Lippmann. The authors included in this analysis were selected because they have been most influential in shaping views of Lippmann within the field of communication; new electronic databases make it possible to identify these patterns of influence.[4]

Inevitably, this endeavor places me in a position of advocacy. This advocacy should not, however, be interpreted as an endorsement of Lippmann's specific prescriptions for the problems of the media or democracy. As he was the first to admit, his prescriptions were always based on analysis of the specific, transient, historical conditions in which problems were enmeshed: to endorse those prescriptions without fresh analysis is to reject both the spirit and method that produced them. For unlike American mass communication research, Lippmann's theory was historicized and his history was theorized.

Mike Dillon suggests a distinction between the "descriptive" and "prescriptive" Lippmann that holds some promise but is ultimately nearly impossible to sustain.[5] My own preference is to recognize, as James Reston did, that the value of Lippmann's work lies in the significance of the questions he raised rather than in the specific answers he gave.[6] His probes identified the fundamental conundrums of modernity, democracy, knowledge, citizenship, and information. My advocacy therefore consists in (1) affirming the value of Lippmann's historically grounded radical questioning; (2) recognizing that many of the questions Lippmann raised remain relevant, even urgent, today; and (3) above all, asserting that the work has not yet received a full or fair hearing in the field because it has been persistently interpreted through the lens of alien epistemological perspectives and agendas.

Lippmann always emphasized method, and his own scholarly method valorized radical openness, a value he acquired from William James. In his first published article as a professional journalist, an obituary for James, Lippmann wrote:

> He was simply open-minded . . . He was willing to listen to what seemed preposterous, and to consider what might, though queer, be true . . . He gave all men and all creeds, any idea, any theory, any superstition, a respectful hearing . . . that he was a man of tolerance never meant the kind of timidity which refuses to take a stand . . . he fought hard for his ideas, because he believed in them . . . And he told his conclusions. He told them, too, without the expert's arrogance toward the man in the street, and without the dainty and finicky horror of being popular or journalistic.[7]

In many different contexts and venues, Lippmann would speak or write about method throughout his life, but openness, risk-taking, reasoned conviction, and intellectual humility remained the touchstones of these efforts.

My advocacy for Lippmann does extend to supporting this approach and these values, and to reassessing his work in light of them.

INTERPRETIVE KNOTS

The plural, knots, is necessary because multiple understandings of Lippmann's work have currency within different quarters of the fragmented field: journalism, "effects" research, propaganda studies, and in the cultural critique of the "effects" tradition. All of these understandings possess an intrinsic logic but few are historically (or even textually) grounded and virtually all fail to position Lippmann's communication-related studies in relation to his larger project or his own well-developed epistemological position.

It is, however, important to recognize that Lippmann's work lends itself to misinterpretation despite—and sometimes because of—his remarkably lucid and engaging writing style. Indeed, even biographers who have done extensive archival research have sometimes been led astray.[8] There are several overlapping reasons for this.

First, Lippmann lived through a period of historical "rupture" and he was exceptionally prescient. He created the modern American vocabulary of political analysis; recognized the limits of the Enlightenment model of the rational man yet remained deeply committed to reason; was the first thinker to apply Freud's ideas to political thought; and developed an epistemology of mass-mediated knowledge, which may only be fully appreciated retroactively in light of the postmodern critique.[9]

Second, he was both very American and deeply cosmopolitan. He has been variously described as "glacial," "antediluvian," a man of "Olympian" detachment, yet, he was thoroughly fluent in the idiom of his day and had an uncanny ability to probe the shadowy recesses of the American psyche: to give voice to the angst of the collective consciousness and to assess the shifting pathologies of American power.[10] He was always close to centers of power, yet usually served as a gadfly to the powerful. Arthur Schlesinger, Jr., saw Lippmann as always moving away from the popular course: always probing the underside of the dialectic.[11] He was variously a muckraker, progressive, pragmatist, realist, liberal, conservative-liberal, and an incisive critic of the limits of all of these positions.

Third, his antidote for everything from news to freedom was "method," by which he meant disciplined rationality, evidence-based judgments, systematic procedure, experiential learning, accountability, and continued openness to countervailing evidence. He believed the scientific method came closest to realizing these values; however, his understanding of scientific inquiry and authority was nonpositivistic, even humanistic, in a time when logical positivism and scientism were in the ascendancy.[12] Consequently, interpreters often mistakenly filtered his advocacy of method through positivistic lenses, especially in the social sciences.

Fourth, his own, reflectively articulated intellectual method, which combined radical openness and risk-taking with intellectual humility, actually cut deeply against the grain of twentieth-century American positivism and dualism. A. J. Leibling described Lippmann as "the greatest on-the-one-hand-this writer in the world."[13] Lippmann's approach allowed him to change his mind, acknowledge confusion, doubt, and error—in short, to grow. When charged with inconsistency, Lippmann responded that in the search for truth one should not be judged by departures from earlier positions but by how much one learns from experience.[14]

Fifth, he defied standard ideological categorizations. Indeed, he has even been described as "non-ideological."[15] A socialist, as a young man, he was at various times an adviser to and critic of every president from Theodore Roosevelt to Lyndon Johnson. His legacy has admirers and detractors among both liberals and conservatives, although, as we see below, he has become a special pariah to some on the left in recent years as a result of Noam Chomsky's interpretive inversion of Lippmann's analysis of "the manufacture of consent."

Sixth, critics tend to blame the messenger for his disturbing assessment of the viability of participatory democracy in complex societies. Lippmann seemed to anticipate this in his discussion of Machiavelli in *Public Opinion*.[16] Like Machiavelli, who is congenitally misread, Lippmann sought a humanistic solution to the pathologies of power. That is, he was trying to find a way to save democracy, not (as is sometimes claimed) to transcend it.

Seventh, he always distinguished between the reliability of his journalistic claims and his scholarship, citing differences in methods and intent.[17] Readers seldom recognized that distinction. And for good reason: because he sometimes published thematically related collections of his journalistic writings in book form.

Eighth, because of the enormous public influence Lippmann enjoyed during his lifetime, he has attracted extensive biographical attention. This biographical attention has, however, contributed to the eclipse of his reputation. The great commercial success of Ronald Steel's 669-page authorized biography, *Walter Lippmann and the American Century*, which focused primarily on Lippmann's writings on international relations, his interactions with important public figures, and his personal life, while neglecting his more scholarly works, has contributed to a sense that Lippmann has been "done."[18] As a result, two subsequent book-length intellectual biographies, which have addressed the more philosophical aspects of Lippmann's work, have not received the attention they deserve.[19] The net effect seems to be that, in most quarters, he is remembered more for his celebrity, which he deplored, than his ideas.

Finally, the sheer size of the body of work provides formidable challenges for interpreters. It has been estimated that Lippmann published more than ten million words including twenty-six books, well in excess of five thousand columns and editorials, and wrote more than twenty-thousand letters over more than six decades.[20] Nearly a dozen biographies have been published as well as a vast number of shorter profiles and analytical studies; and Lippmann figures prominently in the memoirs of other journalists and public figures. Consequently, even the most dedicated researcher can only sample the work.

Sampling and summarizing Lippmann is, as Theodore Peterson so aptly notes, like "describing the Grand Canyon as a magnificent example of soil erosion."[21] Context, nuance, the ever-present qualifying "other-hand" on which so much depends, and the luminous eloquence of the prose, are lost. Assessing his contributions without reference to the philosophical perspective which motivated it, is equally misleading.

COSMOPOLITANISM

The essential key to interpreting Lippmann's work is his cosmopolitan perspective and theory of history. Cosmopolitanism informs his view of science, explains his ideological complexity, and structures his analytic framework. According to D. Stephen Blum, "prevailing interpretations of Lippmann's thought ... have been restrictive, even simplistic" because they have failed to take his cosmopolitanism seriously. "The most favored interpretive device," according to Blum, "has been the indictment of inconsistency, the charge that he was something of an ideological vagabond who drifted from one political or philosophical position to the next, thereby sacrificing overall coherence and purpose."[22]

Blum argues that by virtue of Lippmann's unusual background, annual educational trips to Europe from early childhood, a precocious adolescent interest in art history, a rigorous classical education, exceptional intelligence, and several extraordinary mentoring experiences, Lippmann not only developed an intellectual catholicity and openness to experience, but that his work was also consistently informed by a cosmopolitan theory of history. That is, he recognized that modernity was radically transforming the social environment in incalculable ways: that changes in economics, political formations, culture and thought, facilitated by new technologies of transport and communication, were producing unprecedented international interdependence. As a result, American provincialism and isolationism were no longer tenable, and potentially dangerous. Blum maintains that the "Great Society" metaphor, which Lippmann borrowed from his mentor and friend Graham Wallas and used throughout his life, is emblematic of the constancy of his commitment to cosmopolitanism.[23]

Historians generally have paid insufficient attention to the role that cosmopolitanism played in twentieth-century American intellectual history, a lapse David Hollinger has identified and tried to remedy.[24] Hollinger points out that cosmopolitanism has been overshadowed by the theme of intellectual and artistic alienation, and by sociological critiques of assimilation, with which cosmopolitanism is mistakenly identified. Cosmopolitanism rejected both the Anglo-Protestant assimilation model and the divisive parochialism of what we would today call identity-politics; it also sought to transcend the bland tolerance of liberal-pluralism. A critical response to the resurgence of nativism that accompanied the great waves of immigration early in the century, cosmopolitanism was an attempt to draw upon the resources of diverse ethnic cultures to create a new, more universalistic outlook.

Cosmopolitanism opened up American intellectual culture to previously marginalized groups, especially Jews and the Irish—intellectuals in flight from "from Moses and Jesus to Venus and Apollo."[25] Henry Ford denounced cosmopolitanism as a "world Jewish conspiracy" because prominent Jewish intellectuals such as Lippmann, Einstein, Paul Rosenfeld, Morris Cohen, Alfred Kazin, and Lionel Trilling were cosmopolitans.[26] Cosmopolitanism provided openings to European critical theory, especially in the 1930s when an Americanized counterpart of socialist realism inspired the documentary and proletarian literature movements that produced the work of Dorothea Lange, James Agree and Walker Evans, Peres Lorenz, John Steinbeck, James T. Farrell, Herbert Gold, and others.[27] Hollinger points out that by 1950 cosmopolitanism all but defined what it meant to be an intellectual in America regardless of ethnicity. Later, some cosmopolitans would abandon or reverse their flight, but others, like Lippmann, continued to contend that there was no turning back, without dire consequences, in an interdependent, nuclear-armed world.

Lippmann's cosmopolitanism has to be understood in relation to his other intellectual sympathies and influences and to his continuous struggles to synthesize those influences, as well as to experiment with new ideas and take into account changing historical circumstances. Some formative influences were Jamesian pragmatism, Santayana's naturalism, Fabian socialism, a Freudian understanding of the irrational, Holmesian realism, and a Progressive belief, shared with figures such as Veblen, Dewey, and others, that knowledge produced by efforts to solve technical problems is more trustworthy than knowledge that is subjected to censorship at the source by commercial, partisan political, or religious interests. For Lippmann, then, cosmopolitanism was a normative alternative to materialism and fundamentalism.[28]

In practice, it meant that he typically focused on large units of analysis—the news, public opinion, the nation, relations among nations—and that he took the long historical view of these constructs. Distrusting concentrations of power, Lippmann sought to counterbalance competing interests in a fractious Great Society: feminism and women's suffrage to counter patriarchy, opportunities for Germany's postwar rehabilitation against Britain and France's imperial ambitions at Versailles in 1919, unionism and industrial democracy to balance expansion of corporate power, Keynesian economics and welfare state safety nets to ameliorate economic inequality, and so on. The defining feature of his political philosophy was the "firm belief that all arbitrary and concentrated power, public or private, needed to be checked."[29] As the balance of power among competing interests shifted, so did Lippmann's prescriptions for rebalancing them. A socialist and member of bohemian circles in the early part of the century when trusts needed busting, in his later years he saw expansion of the middle class as democracy's best hope.

Christopher Lasch considers Lippmann's cosmopolitanism evidence of cultural elitism; to be sure, Lippmann's aesthetic interests, like those of many highly educated people of his generation, favored high rather than popular culture, though he seems to have had more than a passing knowledge of baseball and boxing. Taste cultures and political attitudes are not, however, synonymous; and, all academics, even Lasch, are members of elite intellectual strata by virtue of their educational credentials. Lippmann himself acknowledges this kind of elitism: borrowing from Socrates, he points out that skepticism is only possible when one is free of hunger, pain, and fear. The political implications of Lippmann's analysis of public opinion pose deeper questions about elitism, especially among contemporary American political scientists and political activists who interpret his sociology of knowledge as a challenge to the competence and sovereignty of the American citizen, and even to the viability of democracy. Yet, others regard such readings as profound misunderstandings of Lippmann's deep democratic commitments: indeed, John Dewey anticipated such misinterpretations, and explicitly defended Lippmann against charges of elitism. I share the view of

Dewey and others who maintain that *Public Opinion* was intended as a work of epistemology, not as an apology for elite values; however, the consequence of Lippmann's epistemological diagnosis leads almost inevitably to the conclusion of *The Phantom Public* that in a large and complex modern country, leaders must rely on the technical knowledge of experts to govern effectively.[30]

PHILOSOPHER IN THE NEWS ROOM

Lippmann was a brilliant student at Harvard, personally mentored by William James, George Santayana, and Graham Wallas. He was expected to follow in their footsteps, but he found the prospect of teaching the same courses year-after-year deadening, and decided to pursue a life of action instead. He learned journalism under the direct tutelage of muckraker Lincoln Steffens, briefly served as secretary to the socialist mayor of Schenectady, New York; was a founding editor of the *New Republic*, then an army propagandist and intelligence officer who helped write Woodrow Wilson's Fourteen Points during World War I; and finally settled into a distinguished career as an editor, political columnist, and public philosopher.

For Lippmann, the practical worlds of politics and journalism were laboratories for testing his philosophical ideas. As the raw material of history shifted during his long sojourn from the horse-and-buggy age to the space age, so did his conclusions. His major analyses of journalism and democracy, *Liberty and the News* (1919–1920), "A Test of the News" (1920), *Public Opinion* (1922), and *The Phantom Public* (1925), were written while he was still a young man, although he continued to address the questions these works raised throughout his life, and to revise his responses to them. John Luskin's *Lippmann, Liberty, and the Press* (1972) tracks Lippmann's evolving views on the press from the early works through his "summing" up in a colloquy at Columbia University in 1969 where, though somber and skeptical, he retained what Luskin and others consider his most remarkable quality: his "openness of mind."[31]

In theory, *Liberty and the News* is Lippmann's seminal contribution to journalism and journalistic studies. The reality, however, is that the model of Lippmann's illustrious career, his advocacy on behalf of the profession, and the fog of misunderstandings about journalistic objectivity that have been attached to his name and reproduced by journalistic educators have been far more influential than any sustained engagements with his theoretical texts by journalism scholars. To be sure, inspiring quotes are often cribbed from his work for ceremonial occasions: perhaps none more frequently than his description of the newspaper as "the bible of democracy."[32] He is ritualistically honored as the "patron saint of modern journalism" as, for example, in David Halberstam's plaudit that Lippmann "shaped a generation. By his presence he made the profession infinitely more respectable, infinitely more honorable, and that much more, in fact, a true profession."[33]

It is relatively easy to expose the interpretive limits of journalism's renderings of Lippmann's legacy, but probably impossible ever to dislodge them. As the lore of journalism claims, Lippmann did contribute to and even to a considerable degree spearhead the movement to professionalize journalism through both advocacy and example. Before he took up the cause, however, the movement was already underway: journalism education began earlier in the century and journalism textbooks were already available. Although Lippmann strongly endorsed more education for journalists, he expressed uncertainty about the value of journalism schools in providing that education.

In 1919 Lippmann's conception of professionalism and the "disinterestedness" that it was supposed to promote was very different from present understandings of these constructs. Historian Thomas L. Haskell has examined theories of professionalism from the period and has shown that within the specific social conditions of the time "professionalism appeared to be a promising corrective, or even antithesis, to capitalism."[34] Indeed Haskell maintains that until the rise of totalitarianism in the 1930s, "virtually all thinking Americans" believed that "professionalism offered a way of life morally superior to the marketplace" because professionals were held accountable to nonpecuniary standards by their peers.[35] Today, of course, many professionals are enthusiastic capitalists: the grain of truth that survives from the earlier period is that in addition to responding to the market, professionals are also accountable to their fields' standards of practice including technical expertise, codes of ethics, and peer review as well as educational and licensing requirements. Like other "thinking Americans" after World War II, Lippmann recognized the failure of professionalism to realize its earlier promise, including the displacement of the disinterested search for truth in journalism by personal ambition.

The term "disinterested," which Lippmann and his peers frequently used during that period, has also lost its earlier meaning.[36] During the Progressive Era, it simply meant not advancing a claim on behalf of "the interests." In that context, interests typically referred to business (the trusts) and politics (political machines), but interests could also mean special pleadings on behalf of class, religion, tribe, region, and so on. In recommending disinterestedness as an ascetic discipline for journalists, Lippmann was not recommending neutrality or indifference, but rather a passionate attachment to the honest (open) pursuit of truth despite the risks and obstacles that stand in its way.[37]

Among Progressives, "disinterested" was so widely used that it did not require explanation in 1919. "Interest" is not, however, synonymous with "bias," as that term is used today in naïve criticisms of media, to imply that unbiased news is possible. To Lippmann and the pragmatists, all claims, including disinterested ones, were social constructs. Truth was understood as contingent, defined in probabilistic, or for C.S. Peirce, communitarian terms; nevertheless, Lippmann retained the hope that lies, misrepresentations, publicity, and propaganda put forth on behalf of "interests" could be identified and exposed. Indeed, he maintained, "There can be no liberty for a community which lacks the information by which to detect lies."[38]

Lippmann fully understood that news is made, not found; and that all reporting is necessarily selective. He did not use the term "objectivity" in *Liberty and the News*; however, he did leave openings within the fabric of the text that could be used to advance the "strategic ritual" of objectivity.[39] Whether Lippmann can be seen as an advocate of objectivity as some claim or an agnostic as others contend depends on how one understands objectivity, truth, and facts.

It is, however, possible to claim, without equivocation, that Lippmann did not approach objectivity as a naïve realist; and that he would regard standards of objectivity invoked by most journalism textbooks and practiced in newsrooms today as naïve. These standards assume a relatively uncomplicated relationship between event and account—whereas the whole point of Lippmann's reflections on the press is to demonstrate how intractably complex that relationship is.

His understanding of "objective" reporting is historical; in this regard, it is largely consonant with Dan Schiller's analysis of the development of the objective press.[40] That is, it refers to the emergence of fact- (even data-) based reporting. In Lippmann's view, the press in America had successfully emancipated itself from political control, only to be subordinated to crass commercial imperatives. The result was the "yellow press," which would produce any sensation that would sell; however, Lippmann maintained that the yellow press contained "within itself the seeds of its own dissolution" because it failed to put events in context or interpret them in ways that could be verified by subsequent events.[41] That is, it provided romantic fictions and entertainments, rather than the reliable accounts of social reality that modern readers needed. As a result, Lippmann maintained that a "new journalism" had emerged in the 1920s that demonstrated that "the objective, orderly, and comprehensive presentation of news is a far more successful type of journalism to-day than the dramatic, disorderly, episodic type."[42] Lippmann thought the objective press was freer from hidden control by the "interests" as well as from attempts by publishers and reporters to exploit the whims of the public.

He maintained—and this is a crucial qualifier—that

> the ability to present news objectively and to interpret it realistically is not a native instinct in the human species; it is a product of culture which comes only with knowledge of the past and acute awareness of how deceptive is our normal observation and how wishful is our thinking.[43]

That is, for Lippmann, journalistic objectivity is a cultural practice. The journalist, like all other humans, only sees the reflections on the wall of Plato's cave; the best he or she can offer is "candid and critical observation sought with humility and detachment."[44] This is not the "god's eye" objectivity of positivism and empiricism, but a very human effort to provide historically informed, reflexive interpretations of events. At best, it is an embrace of a "limited objectivity," which possesses strong affinities to contemporary forms of critical realism.[45]

Even this limited objectivity has to be understood within the context of Lippmann's sociology of knowledge. Lippmann's definition of truth is functional, not ontological: "the function of truth is to bring to light the hidden facts, to set them into relation with each other, and make a picture of reality on which men can act."[46] For Lippmann truth is provisional, always open to new evidence provided by changing realities: in 1911, he wrote, "Truths are like the clothes of a growing boy, not like the shroud of a corpse."[47] Conversely, he claimed, "the function of news is to signalize an event."[48] According to Lippmann, truth and news coincide in only a small portion of the field of human interest, and then only where "social conditions take recognizable and measurable shape."[49] Truth, then, has an "uncertain character."[50] Truth and facts are social: they are only as reliable (actionable) as the institutions that produce them.

Facts are artifacts of institutional record keeping.[51] The press relies on social institutions to keep these records: to provide facts. The journalist's task is to put the facts together and to interpret them. Lippmann draws an analogy between putting a jigsaw puzzle together and preparing a news report: the pieces will only fit together if they have been crafted with precision. It is the task of social institutions to provide the knowledge base upon which the press depends: "At its best the press is a servant and guardian of institutions; at its worst it is a means by which a few exploit social disorganization to their own ends."[52] Lippmann attributed the failures of the press, especially its vulnerability to "the orgy of lying which war propaganda let loose" during World War I, to the failure of democratic social institutions to furnish themselves with adequate "instruments of knowledge."[53]

It is within the context of this failure that he recommends creation of "intelligence bureaus."[54] His hope was that the reliability of fact-based news reporting could be improved by the creation of an array of knowledge centers, including quasigovernmental agencies, independent research institutes, and university research centers, which would generate and analyze information that legislators, administrators, and journalists could draw upon. Lippmann called on the press to reform itself as well by measures such as self-policing through the creation of "courts of honor," developing standards of admissibility for eye-witness accounts similar to those used in courts, and making false documentation illegal.[55]

Lippmann is far more confident in describing untruth—lies, propaganda, publicity—than truth. He acknowledges this, and expresses a pragmatist's hope in *Liberty and the News* that method will show the way in the future. In the meantime, truth is to be understood more as a journey than a destination: for reporters, it involves a willingness to be fired rather than write what they do not believe. For scholars, it means taking a longer view, by providing expert knowledge, "intelligence," which through communal processes of criticism and self-correction, becomes increasingly more reliable. Lippmann's youthful hope, which was directly influenced by Peirce, was that methods of intelligence would eventually be perfected to the point where various forms of knowledge would converge.[56] He regarded freedom of expression (liberty) to be a necessary precondition to this convergence. The mature Lippmann was less hopeful about the prospects for convergence.

Overall, Lippmann's elevated status within the folklore of journalism is only loosely based in his texts. Much seems to depend on strategic attachments to his coattails, his celebrity, career model, and advocacy for the profession. Journalistic lore has dehistoricized his approach to objectivity, extricated it from its epistemological grounding, and translated it into a series of formulaic practices that not only do not conform to the letter but also betray the spirit of his intent. That is, it has turned objectivity into professional cant: a shield to protect journalism from criticism.[57] Those who seek to implode the tarnished idol of journalistic objectivity to emancipate truth will actually find more in Lippmann's writings on the press to support their quest than to oppose it.

RECEPTION OF LIPPMANN WITHIN THE "EFFECTS TRADITION" OF COMMUNICATION RESEARCH

Lippmann is arguably the most important single figure in the immediate prehistory of academic communication research. The late James W. Carey, who did so much to inspire interest in histories of media and media research, thought that a responsible revisionary history needed to foreground Lippmann. Carey wrote:

> Walter Lippmann's *Public Opinion* (1922) is, I believe, the founding book in American media studies. It was not the first book written about the mass media in America, but it was the first serious work to be philosophical and analytical in confronting the mass media. The title of the book may be *Public Opinion*, but its subject and central actor is the mass media, particularly the news media. The book founded or at least clarified a continuous tradition of research as well. Finally, the book self-consciously restated the central problematic in the study of mass media.[58]

As we shall see later, Lippmann was not the hero of Carey's own revisionary narrative, even though he was a central player.

Lippmann's position in the field of communication research was, however, established long before Carey addressed it. He was there from the beginning. The success of his books, including the controversies they created as well as his considerable public influence, helped cultivate an intellectual climate in which studies of public opinion, mass media, and propaganda assumed significance, respectability, and urgency.

Wilbur Schramm, who virtually defined what would become the dominant paradigm in the field for the next three decades, included a chapter from Lippmann's *Public Opinion* in one of the field's first textbook, *Mass Communications* (1949); Schramm and Donald Roberts would also include the chapter, "The World Outside and the Pictures in Our Heads," in revised editions of *The Process and Effects of Mass Communication* (1971), which was for many years the best-selling and by far the most influential textbook in the field.[59]

Since Lippmann was a journalist, not a behavioral scientist, he did not qualify for elevation to the status of a "founder" of the field in Schramm's book. Presumably for the same reason, Lippmann did not even qualify as a "forefather" in Schramm's posthumously published *The Beginnings of Communication Study in America*.[60] Lippmann's work did, however, exercise traceable influence over two of Schramm's four founders, Paul Lazarsfeld and Harold Lasswell. Lazarsfeld praised Lippmann's work; and Lasswell built directly upon it, endowing it with the Machiavellian twist that Lippmann had explicitly rejected.[61]

Schramm did not offer significant commentary on Lippmann's work; his influence over the assimilation of Lippmann's ideas into the effects tradition was a simple extension of his own influence as institution builder and author of the legitimating narrative of effects research. That is, he entered Lippmann's name into the discourse, established his relevance, and linked him, by association, with the effects tradition.

To be sure, Lippmann was very interested in the effects of mediation, although he conceived of them far more broadly than Schramm and his four founders. Moreover, Lippmann's non-positivistic understanding of the nature and limits of scientific inquiry, articulated most fully in *Drift and Mastery* (1914), is antithetical to the kind of reductive, ahistorical and atheoretical empiricism and scientism that is associated with the "effects" tradition of communication research pioneered by Schramm.

Despite the epistemological incongruity, *Public Opinion* exercised a generative influence over effects research. Lippmann has been described as "the intellectual father of agenda-setting" research, which had produced more than 350 empirical studies as of 2002.[62] He did not use that label, but he did present the idea; and agenda-setting researchers fully acknowledge their debts to Lippmann.[63] Lippmann also described in detail the gatekeeping role of editors.[64] According to the *Oxford English Dictionary*, Lippmann coined the modern usage of the word, "stereotype"; he also developed the concept and even extended it to the analysis of ethnic and class prejudice.[65] Gordon Allport expanded Lippmann's theory in *The Nature of Prejudice* (1954), a work that is generally regarded as the foundational study in the social psychology of prejudice.[66] Effects research, in turn, imported the concept back into communication where it has been widely used in content analysis of media representations of race, gender, age, and other "variables." Lippmann also examined processes of personal influence by opinion leaders, although he did not use the phrase: to my knowledge, he has not been credited with this idea, even though Lazarsfeld and Katz do categorize him as one, "a Great Disseminator," in *Personal Influence*.[67] There are anticipations of uses and gratifications theory in Lippmann's work, although he strongly criticized displacement of civil society by consumerism. His argument that "censorship operates by congestion," along with his analyses of cognitive and technologically conditioned limits ("blindspots") in knowledge, also anticipates George Gerbner's "General Model of Communication."[68] In addition, Lippmann and his colleague, Charles Merz, pioneered the development of content analysis and identified some of its methodological strengths and limits in "A Test of the News," although this achievement has until recently been largely ignored.[69]

Lippmann's books and columns were so widely read during the six decades of his career that many ideas that he put into circulation became part of the common culture. Moreover, he was not only a great disseminator but also a great synthesizer, so that too much originality can easily be attributed to his work. Nevertheless, it is possible to locate many concepts and theoretical insights in his work, which would later gain currency in sociology, political science, and media studies. Because he lacked the benediction of an academic position, it is accurate to say that he was not cited as frequently as he should have been, especially by scholars eager to affirm their membership in the behavioral science fraternity.

Effects research forced Lippmann's ideas into an epistemological straitjacket that he would have rejected; however, it provided empirical support for many of his ideas; and some researchers, who formally reside in the effects camp, have provided richer interpretive accounts than strict adherence to behaviorist methodologies permits.

PROPAGANDA STUDIES

Nowhere is Lippmann's legacy more contentiously debated and gratuitously betrayed than in propaganda studies. I include public relations under the tent of propaganda since the so-called father of public relations, Edward Bernays, did so. Bernays also played a crucial role in corrupting Lippmann's ideas and the interpretive legacy that has developed around them in propaganda studies.[70]

Bernays published *Crystallizing Public Opinion* (1923) the year after Lippmann's *Public Opinion*; and he always claimed that Lippmann provided the theory while he provided the practice.[71] From the beginning, however, Bernays inverted Lippmann's arguments, twisting criticism into advocacy. Where Lippmann saw truth and liberty imperiled "in a time when the manufacture of consent is an unregulated private enterprise," Bernays saw opportunity.[72]

Bernays's enterprise, public relations, was dedicated to the manufacture of consent on behalf of the "interests" that Lippmann and the Progressives had sought to constrain. In Lippmann's view, liberty is a precondition to the search for truth; and censorship and propaganda are interdependent forces that abridge liberty. For Bernays propaganda is a useful tool. Contra Lippmann, Bernays writes:

> Mr. Lippmann says propaganda is dependent on censorship. From my point of view the precise reverse is more nearly true. Propaganda is a purposeful directed effort to overcome censorship—the censorship of the group mind and the herd reaction.[73]

The role of the public relations practitioner in Bernays's formulation is to direct the propaganda effort.

Lippmann was scathingly critical of public relations in *Public Opinion*, describing the publicity man as follows: "He is a censor and a propagandist, responsible only to his employers, and to the whole truth responsible only as it accords with the employers' conception of his own interests."[74] To Lippmann, publicity agents are architects of "pseudo-environments," who work actively to plant or distort the pictures in our heads, and to circumvent journalists' access to direct channels of news.[75] In short, for Lippmann, public relations is the problem; for Bernays, it is the solution. The difference could not be clearer to anyone who seriously consults the original texts.

As has already been intimated, Harold Lasswell accomplishes a similar inversion in *Propaganda Technique in the World War* (1927). Lasswell does not directly cite Lippmann, although he does refer to the existence of a literature on public opinion "of such an abstruse and indefinite character that it defies empirical verification."[76] It is, however, widely assumed that Lippmann exercised significant influence over Lasswell's thinking.

In a replay of the Bernays's script, Lippmann offered the diagnosis—propaganda abridges democracy—and, to quote Christopher Simpson, "Lasswell extended the idea, giving it a Machiavellian twist."[77] In Lasswell's own words, he sought to "evolve an explicit theory of how international war propaganda may be conducted with success."[78] In many subsequent interpretations in propaganda studies, the analyses of Lippmann and Lasswell have been conflated. Lippmann, who wrote three books in response to "the orgy of lying which war propaganda let loose," is somehow reread as an advocate of propaganda.[79]

How can this be explained?

Lippmann's biography is a contributing factor. Like his work, it is frequently misinterpreted. Lippmann was an intelligence officer and a propagandist during the war. His assignment as an intelligence officer consisted in working in secret to articulate the terms of the U.S. peace plan for ending the war. In that capacity, he advised the War Department, "We should avoid all the tricky and sinister aspects of what is usually called propaganda, and should aim to create the impression that here is something new [The League of Nations] and infinitely hopeful in the affairs of mankind."[80] His work as a propaganda officer consisted in writing leaflets encouraging German soldiers to surrender.

Lippmann was not a member of George Creel's Committee on Public Information (CPI).[81] The leaflet program was deliberately kept out of Creel's hands by Secretary of War Newton Baker, who was not about to cede battlefield strategy to the civilian propaganda czar.[82] Moreover, Lippmann would have never have enlisted in a program affiliated with the CPI. He had been a vehement critic of Creel before the war, calling him a "reckless and incompetent person" in an editorial in the *New Republic*. In response to Creel's attempt to ban socialist publications in 1917, Lippmann approached Supreme Court Justice Brandeis and later Colonial House (Wilson's chief advisor) to try to stop the suppression. Lippmann continued to criticize the Creel Commission within official channels throughout the war; and after the war he wrote a scathing postmortem for the the *New Republic* describing the CPI's propaganda efforts as one of "the great calamities" of the war.[83]

Additional biographical factors that may lead some interpreters to equate Lippmann and Lasswell's approaches to propaganda include (1) the fact that for almost sixty years, as editor, columnist, author of books, public figure, and advisor to presidents, Lippmann actively sought to influence public opinion; and, following William James's example, he took strong stands on public issues and "fought hard for his ideas because he believed in them"; (2) throughout his life, he advocated strong leadership; and (3) perhaps above all, as a young man, he was a political activist, even a leading figure in the Progressive movement; and like other Progressives, including Herbert Croly and Walter Weyl (his co-editors at the *New Republic*), John Dewey, Jane Addams, Lester Ward, E.A. Ross, and others, Lippmann was always deeply concerned with the problem of social control—what Robert Wiebe calls "the search for order."[84]

This aspect of the Progressive movement often puzzles contemporary thinkers who are attracted by many of the ideals of the Progressives. The late nineteenth and early twentieth century was a period of great turbulence and rupture. The progressives feared that the great gulf dividing the rich and poor—the "Robber Barons" and the "teeming masses"—would lead to either tyrannical oppression from above or revolution from below. Moreover, the background influences of the Civil War and Reconstruction on these thinkers should not be ignored; the older members of the Progressive generation, like Dewey, were children during that period.[85] They shared the conviction that American democracy was fragile and could fracture again. Progressive reform was a both/and proposition: spurred by commitments to social justice as well as more conservative concerns for stability and order.

Lippmann's solution to the problem of social control, technocracy, is not a solution contemporary advocates of social justice can support. Nevertheless it should not be confused with either Bernays's or Lasswell's solutions, which are arguably the solutions that have prevailed. Lippmann's technocratic experts and insiders were supposed to generate "disinterested" knowledge and use it to promote the public good. His view of technology also had a democratic, moral dimension. When, for example, Stuart Chase, in runaway enthusiasm for technology, embraced the technological imperative as "impersonal, amoral, and nonethical," Lippmann responded:

> Have not technicians . . . been relieved of all restraint? If the technological impera-
> tives of his [Chase's] technocrats are so impersonal, so amoral, and so non-ethical,
> then how can they ever be challenged? Against these imperatives there are no human
> rights, not even the right of revolution.[86]

Moreover, Lippmann's technocracy was meritocratic. Expertise was achieved through effort, intelligence, and education (the American dream); and Lippmann supported universal access to public education. Today meritocracy, universal public education, and the American dream carry more ideological weight than persuasive power. Presumably, however, contemporary social justice movements are still motivated, as Lippmann was, by efforts to translate these ideals into reality even though we no longer share the Progressives' faith in experts.

Even more perplexing than Bernays's and Lasswell's inversions is the careless interpretation of Lippmann put forth by Noam Chomsky, who is a careful scholar when operating within his own area of expertise. In a chapter in *Media Control* (1991) titled "Spectator Democracy," Chomsky refers to the subtitle (he does not provide a title) of a work by Lippmann as "something like 'A Progressive Theory of Liberal Democratic Thought' [*sic*]."[87] He then provides a series of phrases in quotation marks with no page numbers or additional sourcing; the phrases are "revolution in the art of democracy," "manufacture of consent," "the common interests elude public opinion entirely," "specialized class," and "responsible men." He fills in the blanks in between these phrases with incendiary claims and describes the result as "a typical Leninist view." Two pages later Chomsky adds three more phrases, "the bewildered herd," "functions," and "spectators," to his concordance to Lippmann. He follows these with two more statements in quotations, which he attributes to the members of the bewildered herd who inhabit Lippmann's Leninist state: "they are allowed to say, 'We want you to be our leader' or 'We want *you* to be our leader.'"[88]

Yes, Chomsky is doing politics here, not scholarship. He is constructing a straw man, so that he can blow him away, and use the rest of the book to develop his own critical takes on international politics. In fact, however, Lippmann, the villain of the narrative, actually agreed with some of Chomsky's views on foreign policy, including criticisms of U.S. imperialism in Central America, the immorality of the Vietnam War, and the Manichean framing of the Russians during the cold war. The petard has been hoisted, and the exercise could be dismissed accordingly, except for the fact that Chomsky's view of Lippmann has far more currency, as measured by citations, within current scholarship than any other single individual cited in this chapter except Lippmann's biographer, Ronald Steel.[89] Chomsky's collaborative effort with Edward Herman, which is a work of scholarship as well as politics, *Manufacturing Consent: The Political Economy of Mass Media* (1988), borrows its title from Lippmann. Lippmann is credited in a footnote to the Preface, but is not discussed elsewhere, so that book is not examined here.

The interpretive conundrum for media studies scholars, who identify with critical traditions, is compounded further by Stuart Ewen's take on Lippmann in *PR!: A Social History of Spin* (1996). Part of the book involves archival research on the origins of the public relations industry; and it is one of the best critical sources on Bernays. Yet, the interpretation of Lippmann is deeply problematic despite the fact that Ewen does cite textual sources and consult Steel's biography. In my view, Ewen's account goes astray for two reasons.

First, and foremost, because of the direct agency of Edward Bernays himself, who Ewen interviewed: reporting on the interview, Ewen writes, "I was particularly intrigued, for example, by Bernays's reflections on the connection between his thinking and that of Walter Lippmann."[90] Those connections, as Bernays's interpreted them, set the agenda for and guide Ewen's reading of Lippmann. In fact, Ewen pushes Bernays's inversion even farther. The reader is encouraged to go to the source for full verification; length limits me to only a few examples from about fifty pages of references to Lippmann, all of a similar flavor. Bernays tells Ewen:

> Lippmann treated public opinion on a purely theoretical basis. He never got down to matters of changing it. He talked of it as if he were a sociologist discussing a social caste system ... abstractly. And I was surprised. Here he was, a working newspaper man.[91]

Exactly! Lippmann was presenting a scholarly analysis of an epistemological and political problem in *Public Opinion*. Now consider these interpretive claims Ewen makes about Lippmann:

> Developing ideas that would become the twentieth century public relations cate-chism, Lippmann cautioned that to govern the way that the press will cover an event, access to that event must be consciously restricted. [Quotation Lippmann] "A group of men who can prevent access to the event" are in a position to "arrange news of it to suit their purposes."[92]

> For Lippmann, the appeal of symbols was that they provided a device for short-cir-cuiting the inconvenience posed by critical reason and public discussion.[93]

> Appeals to reason were not merely discarded as futile; they were being consciously undermined to serve the interests of power.[94]

Substitute Bernays for Lippmann in these quotes, and they become more accurate renderings. Restore the context to the Lippmann quote in the first statement and it is clear that Lippmann is criticizing, not advocating, the restriction of access to the press by publicity men.

Bernays's inversion of Lippmann not only survives Ewen's rereading; Ewen amplifies it. No one who reads Lippmann *qua* Lippmann would ever claim that he sought to short-circuit critical reason. Lippmann was a lifelong advocate of critical reason and he always recommended it to journalists and scholars, and to the wide array of public groups he spoke to, from the Women's City Club of New York to the United Nations.

Second, Ewen interprets Lippmann through the reflecting mirror of his own well-developed theory of the power of images. Ewen reports that, "From the van-tage point of the 1990s, one cannot avoid being struck by Lippmann's clairvoy-ance; the extent to which his analysis of symbols—how they may be employed to sway the public—sounds uncomfortably familiar"[95]—familiar not only because it is the world we inhabit, but also because it is a world that Ewen (like Lippmann) criticized so incisively in his own books. Rather than being prophetic, however, Ewen concludes that in the 1920s, Lippmann's analysis would have been received as "prescriptive."[96] That is, Ewen holds Lippmann responsible for creating the world that he (Ewen) analyzes in *PR!*.

Ewen's interest in visual images is projected onto Lippmann's argument. In Ewen's interpretation, Lippmann's "pictures in our heads" seem to become literal images rather than cognitive mapping of ideas and concepts. Lippmann's "news" and "the press" become Ewen's "mass communication, particularly the cinema" and "new media."[97] In *Public Opinion*, Lippmann does make five incidental ref-erences to "the moving pictures," an industry that was still taking form when Lippmann wrote *Public Opinion*. Lippmann's comments are prescient, but he does not analyze film, per se: his longest reference to film is less than a paragraph. Ewen's discussion of Lippmann's view of film is more expansive than the original; and it is framed in language and concepts that were not available to Lippmann in 1922. For example, Ewen writes, "Lippmann turned to Hollywood, America's 'dream factory,' for inspiration," and "Hollywood, Lippmann observed, routinely achieved this state of being [cathexis]."[98] Ewen further contends that, "Inspired by the example of Hollywood, Lippmann began to envision game plans for persuasion that, though novel within his world, are today standard practices."[99] In fact, Lippmann *never* refers to Hollywood in *Public Opinion*. The film industry had only relocated from New Jersey to Hollywood in 1911; there was nothing "routine" about it yet; and, moreover, it would be almost thirty more years before anthropologist Hortense Powdermaker would christen *Hollywood: The Dream Factory* (1950).

While we can never fully escape the captivity of our own time, location, and priorities, Stephen Toulmin warns that in doing historical analyses, we need to make every effort to see the world through our subjects' "horizons of expectations," not our own: those horizons mark the boundaries of what seems possible or feasible within a field of action at a given moment in time.[100] Even if, as Ewen seems determined to believe, Lippmann had been an advocate of the "manufacture of consent" by PR rather than its critic, Hollywood was not the center of gravity of American culture in 1922. Lippmann was a man of letters, deeply invested in the power of print; the focus of *Public Opinion* is news and political knowledge, not entertainment.

Lippmann does recognize the significance of symbols—tangible images such as flags, uniforms, and coins—and he discusses some of the ways they have been used to deceive as well as to arouse the public for prosocial purposes. This is elementary sociology, well established in the nineteenth century by founders of the field such as Durkheim, Weber, Simmel, and others, not an original contribution. Lippmann describes "the manufacture of consent" as an old art, "one which was supposed to die out with the appearance of democracy," but has not.[101] Its survival is the reason why Lippmann believes that we—scholars, journalists, administrators, and citizens—need to develop a new critical awareness of how our images of unseen worlds are formed. To this end, in a chapter in *Public Opinion* titled "The Appeal to the Public," he provides teachers with a series of strategies to use "to make the pupil acutely aware of how the mind works on unfamiliar facts"—what we would today call strategies for media literacy or critical thinking.[102] If, as Ewen contends, Lippmann's objective was to short-circuit critical reason to facilitate elite rule, why would he want to equip the young with critical reasoning skills?[103]

In the sequel to *Public Opinion*, *The Phantom Public*, Lippmann would be more pessimistic about citizens' interest in and ability to participate effectively in public affairs. He contended that, at best, citizens could develop competence in a few areas of interest or expertise. In making these claims about the complexity of modern knowledge and cognitive limits of citizens, however, Lippmann always emphasized that he too was vulnerable to these limits: a point that even friendly readers tend to ignore.

CULTURAL CRITIQUE OF THE EFFECTS TRADITION

As we have seen, James Carey considers *Public Opinion* to be "the founding book in American media studies," but he regards this as an unfortunate development. His nominee for foundational thinker is John Dewey, who Carey believes could have inspired a tradition in communication studies that would be more original, continuously creative, socially relevant, and humane.

Dewey and Lippmann's respective intellectual journeys overlapped at several points. Both attracted William James's interest early in their careers and were given encouragement and support by him. Lippmann's *Drift and Mastery* (1914) was influenced by Dewey as well as James; in 1915, Lippmann wrote a short essay on Dewey, "The Footnote," in which he affirmed and expanded on Dewey's call for an antifoundational philosophy based on experience. Conversely, Dewey published articles on public affairs in the the *New Republic* while Lippmann was an editor of the magazine; and Dewey borrowed the Wallas's Great Society metaphor from Lippmann. The two men were frequent allies in political struggles, and during the Progressive Era, they shared similar views of method, social control, efficiency, and social science.[104]

Within the field of communication research, however, interest in the relationship of the two thinkers understandably focuses on a short interlude in their long acquaintance: the five year period that included Lippmann's publication of *Public Opinion* (1922) and *The Phantom Public* (1925), Dewey's reviews of the two books in the *New Republic* (1922 and 1925), and Dewey's lectures at Kenyon College (1926) which were published as *The Public and its Problems* (1927). Dewey's lectures expand on Lippmann's thesis, and probe its pessimistic implication for the future of participatory democracy, which Dewey, like Lippmann, found deeply disturbing. Whether this episode adds up to a controversy between adversaries or, as Peter Simonson describes it, "an ongoing intramural debate within the tradition" of pragmatism, is open to interpretation; in the field of communication, however, the exchange is usually framed as a "conflict."[105]

Carey is responsible for this framing. In crafting it, he does not pretend to offer a systematic historical exegesis of the contributions of Dewey and Lippmann. He states this very directly in the original source, a 1982 essay republished as

"Reconceiving 'Mass' and 'Media'" in *Culture and Communication* (1989): "I will draw out just enough to focus Dewey's conflict with Lippmann and set the stage for the argument I wish to advance."[106] This initial stage-setting takes up only eight pages in a chapter without notes, which includes a long quote from Dewey's *The Public and its Problems* but no direct textual references to *Public Opinion*. Elsewhere, Carey refers back to this text to reiterate and amplify its points. In later work, he develops his interpretation of Dewey more fully, but does not significantly expand his exposition of Lippmann's views.[107] Carey does, however, impute greater agency to Lippmann in the reiterations. In 1996, he writes, "Lippmann, in effect, took the public out of politics and the politics out of public life. In a phrase of the moment, he depoliticized the public sphere."[108]

In the absence of an established tradition of historical analysis in the field, "Reconceiving 'Mass' and 'Media'" has filled the void despite its author's prefatory disclaimer; and it has exercised significant influence in recent years, especially among those who are understandably attracted to Carey's appealing alternative vision for the future of communication studies.[109]

Textually, Lippmann and Dewey function in the chapter as tropes or foils, "stage setters." Carey positions them at opposite points in a fateful fork in the road in early twentieth-century American social thought. Within the economy of Carey's narrative, each carries the full weight of entire philosophical traditions, and Dewey represents the road not taken.

Lippmann is positioned on the dark side—Cartesian, utilitarianism, objectivism, instrumental reason, atomism, positivism, scientism, and pushed to the outer limits, the road to totalitarianism—and when it comes down to disciplines (Carey's original destination) Lippmann becomes the historical precursor of and philosophical standard-bearer for "effects" research. Conversely, Dewey represents pragmatism, democracy, the Chicago School, symbolic interaction, hermeneutics, community, and communication as a humane and humanistic practice in which everyone gets to participate in meaning making. Carey identifies different foundational metaphors framing the two thinkers' conceptions of communication: he characterizes Lippmann's as visual, print-based, representational ("pictures"), monologic, hierarchal, and control-oriented, and Dewey's as auditory (listening), dialogic, interactional, conversational, and democratic.

In Carey's larger argument, Dewey represents the promise of an approach to cultural studies that is rooted in American traditions but open to European thought at those junctures where it can inform understanding of American experience. Carey identifies some European thinkers he believes can speak to and enrich American cultural studies: Hoggart, Williams, Habermas, Foucault, Giddens, and Bourdieu, "but most important yet," the work of Max Weber. He also acknowledges that "Max cannot for long be avoided."[110]

There are good reasons why Carey is attracted to Dewey's pragmatism. Dewey directly defines communication and does so felicitously, placing it in the company of community and communion, where it resonates closely with and provides philosophical groundings for Carey's own "ritual approach" to communication. Carey is not, however, acritical in his embrace of Dewey. He acknowledges that Dewey does not succeed in rescuing democracy from Lippmann's pessimism because Dewey is unable to detach community or the public from face-to-face interaction. Nevertheless, Carey describes Dewey as "one of my heroes, not for any one book or article but for an extended lifetime of courageous public and intellectual service."[111]

Carey's humanistic approach offers a valuable corrective to behaviorism, which in its most extreme forms entirely ignores the pictures in research subjects' heads (subjectivity) in favor of mechanistic models of communication processes. Carey breaks through the silences these models impose and opens up new channels of discourse in the field—a move that enacts his hero's legacy.

In interpreting Lippmann, Carey adopts what Blum calls the "intellectual vagabond" approach. That is, Carey identifies what he regards as a conundrum: that Lippmann's legacy "is still influential, despite the fact that he refuted many of his own views in subsequent works."[112] But Carey does not explore the puzzle (the presumed refutation) further because his purpose is not to analyze Lippmann per se but rather to critique the effects tradition in mass communication research. If Carey had pursued the puzzle to its roots in the original interpretive error of the effects tradition, his devastating critique of that tradition would have been even more powerful.

If the young author of *Public Opinion* is understood as a self-critical pragmatist and Progressive, which was Lippmann's self-understanding in 1922 and the identity that historians and philosophers ascribe to him, then there are critical points of convergence with Carey's position. Carey praises the first generation of progressive intellectuals because "they managed to produce in pragmatism a peculiarly American, antifoundational and antiessential, philosophy."[113] Lippmann shared that philosophy and praised James and Dewey for their contributions to it, although he struggled throughout his life against the relativism that it engendered. Carey acknowledges that, "We [Americans] have always had a problem of scale. The country has always been too large for a democracy or republic."[114] This is Lippmann's premise and point of departure for *Public Opinion* and *The Phantom Public*, which were attempts to resolve the contradiction between ideology and reality by finding a way to ensure as much democracy as possible given America's problems of scale, complexity, heterogeneity, and increasing global interdependence. Carey does not offer a solution for the national dilemma; he does, however, advise more democracy in our immediate environments, specifically in the academic "departments we currently call home."[115] In this suggestion, Carey is true to

Dewey, who made the school classroom his laboratory for democracy.[116] In contrast, Lippmann, the cosmopolitan, saw the nation and the world as the experiential testing ground for his ideas.

The optimistic democratic vistas of Dewey and Carey are, without doubt, far more appealing than the technocratic republic of the young Lippmann's pessimistic prognosis. The author of *Liberty and the News* would surely have preferred them too, but the realist—the self-critical Progressive, pragmatist, and naturalist—could not find a way to take the whole country there. Like Dewey and Carey, he concluded that full participatory democracy is only possible at the local level, where citizens did not need to make decisions about "unseen" environments. Lippmann did not, however, take the public out of politics, though he did consider the Jeffersonian claim that the public can directly govern already obsolete when it was promulgated in the eighteenth century. Yet, even in *The Phantom Public*, Lippmann's most pessimistic book, he saw the public (or public opinion) as playing a crucial role in sustaining American democracy by checking the excesses of insiders (the executive branch and Congress) and resolving legitimating crises. Carey does not, of course, read Lippmann this way.

In a later work, "The Chicago School" (1996), Carey briefly expands on the utilitarian origins of the effects tradition, suggesting that Lippmann served as a linkage between the utilitarian and modern tradition and thereby functioned to short-circuit the more humanistic and distinctly American tradition that absorbed the views of John Milton and J. S. Mill into American culture, producing the Constitution, the Bill of Rights, case law, and the philosophy of freedom. Lippmann, however, directly embraces all of these texts in *Liberty and the News*, although he does criticize the limits of tolerance in Milton (anti-Catholicism) and Mill, who would suppress speech that leads to "mischievous" acts—for example, crimes against property.[117]

Even though Lippmann considers the Constitution a flawed document, it nevertheless assumes paramount importance in his social thought because pragmatism negates ontological first principles; and Lippmann, unlike contemporary pragmatists like Richard Rorty, resists the relativism of antifoundationalism. In the American experience, as Lippmann saw it through a pragmatic lens, the Constitution provides the *social foundation* for American democracy. The tradition of law and procedures it supports, including Holmes's revisionism, is in Lippmann's view, America's best hope for preserving freedom. So much so that in later life Lippmann attempts, unsuccessfully, to locate philosophical grounds in the American experience for reviving the natural rights philosophy of the founders because natural rights theory provided them with a platform for and the courage to revolt against tyranny.[118] I read this as a vibrant extension of the traditions of Milton, Mill, and the founders, not an attempt to bypass them.

Carey also implicates Lippmann in the failure of modern journalism. He maintains that Lippmann ascribes a passive role to journalists as mere "conduits" who "transmit the judgments of experts, and thereby ratify decisions arrived at by that class [experts] not the public or public representatives."[119] That inference can be drawn if *Public Opinion* and *The Phantom Public* are read as utilitarian documents and if *Liberty and the News* is ignored, along with Lippmann's lifelong advocacy on behalf of journalism. Again, however, it is important to remember what Lippmann was writing against early in the twentieth century: a time when the kinds of public information and statistics we take for granted today existed only in rudimentary forms. Lippmann envisioned "disinterested" fact-gathering agencies as informational counterweights that could help journalists expose the lies and hidden manipulations of the yellow press, journalistic fraud, government propaganda, uses of the press as a bully pulpit by publishers and moralists, and stories planted by publicists, politicians, and profiteers—lapses of the press that he explicitly criticized in *Liberty and the News*. In Lippmann's view, the job of the journalist is to exercise skepticism, expose lies, subject eye-witness reports to tests of credibility, and put the pieces of the puzzle (facts) together: that is, to make sense of events and interpret their significance.

This is an active role: one that Lippmann believed required training, experience, and courage. Carey is, however, right: contemporary formulaic versions of journalistic objectivity reduce journalists to passive stenographers of power. This is not, however, the kind of journalism Lippmann advocated or practiced.

Carey's analyses of the problems of contemporary journalism and of the limits of the effects tradition are compelling; my criticism here extends only to his interpretation of Lippmann, which in my judgment stems from a categorical error that Carey inherited from traditions he criticizes. While Carey breaks with the effects tradition, his interpretation of Lippmann is nevertheless consistent with it. By this, I mean that he takes what the effects tradition has made of Lippmann's work at face value. In this respect, Carey leaves the received "wisdom" of the field intact. That is, he sees Lippmann as effects researchers saw him: as one of their own. As we have seen, however, effects research ignored Lippmann's philosophical location and imposed their behaviorist template on his work. Interpreting Lippmann as the effects tradition interpreted him is standard practice in the communication literature and in accounts of communication research; this view of Lippmann is, however, a discipline-specific interpretation, which reflects the powerful hold effects research has had over communication research.

Carey urges those who share his enthusiasm for developing a cultural approach to American communication research to deconstruct radically the effects tradition. Deconstructing the distorted view of Lippmann that we have inherited from that tradition is consistent with this recommendation.

Carey's argument for a cultural approach to communication with American roots has been well received in the field; and his interpretation of Lippmann has significant resonance. To trace all the permutations that resonance has taken would require volumes; however, within that chain of influence, the work of John Durham Peters and Jay Rosen has exercised the most influence.[120] Both built on Carey's dichotomous framing of Dewey and Lippmann.

In his 1989 essay, "Democracy and American Mass Communication Theory: Dewey, Lippmann, Lazarsfeld," Peters paints contrasting portraits of the two thinkers as a prelude to posing an original argument: that much of mass communication research is an attempt to carry out a political project without being articulate about it.[121] It is an important and well-wrought argument despite the fact that, in my judgment, it reduces Lippmann to a stick figure. Peters is less rhapsodic than Carey or Rosen in his treatment of Dewey; but he is even harder on Lippmann in the 1989 formulation where, like Ewen and the later Carey, he seems to impute agency to Lippmann's argument. That is, Lippmann is not treated as a groundbreaking thinker who provides an early diagnosis of the collapse of the public sphere; rather he is implicated in facilitating its evacuation by virtue of what others have made of his work.

Peters has subsequently rethought his position. In 1997, he maintained, "Dewey wasn't so right and Lippmann wasn't so wrong"; and in *Speaking into the Air: A History of the Idea of Communication* (1999), Peters critiqued dialog as a model for democratic communication in the nation-state, and replaced it with dissemination.[122] However, his earlier position on Lippmann remains influential. In Peters's 1989 essay, as in Carey's work, both Dewey and Lippmann lift heavy weights. The two thinkers not only represent different philosophies—this time Dewey as an Aristotelian and Lippmann as a Platonist—but also different generations.[123] Dewey carries the banner of the Progressive Era, 1890s–1920s while Lippmann wears the badge of value-free, scientific research that took hold later. Lippmann is again saddled with the responsibility for the effects tradition: "American mass communication theory and research, at least in its theoretical vision, is a series of footnotes to Lippmann's *Public Opinion*."[124] Once more Dewey gets to claim the legacy of James and Peirce, while Lippmann is orphaned. Lippmann is also cut off from the Progressive movement, even though he was a founding editor of the *New Republic*, which was regarded as a quasi-official voice of Progressivism. While Carey is critical of Peters's 1989 essay, I find Peters's portrayals of Dewey and Lippmann to be more nuanced, but on balance, consistent with Carey's interpretation.[125]

My positioning of Rosen in this section of the chapter is a stretch. He is influenced by the Lippmann-Dewey exchange, including among other influences Carey's interpretation of it, and even more directly by Carey's cultural approach itself; however, the effects tradition has no real bearing on his activist project,

"public journalism." Rosen freely acknowledges his debts to Carey, whose journalistic ideals do seem to be inspired more by Dewey's "courage" and his faith
in democracy than by the contents of *The Public and its Problems*.[126] Exploration
of public journalism per se lies outside of the scope of this chapter. For our very
limited purpose, Rosen's work is of relevance as a channel for reproducing and
amplifying Carey's interpretation of Lippmann. That is, the considerable success
of Rosen's work has further entrenched the view of Lippmann as a representative
of utilitarianism and scientism as well as a philosophical opponent of participatory democracy and an intellectual nomad.

CONCLUSION: HERMENEUTIC GOLDEN RULE

Deconstruction is a dirty business especially when applied to the texts of thinkers
one admires. No text is impervious to it. To get our work done, we must all make
interpretive leaps. I certainly do that here.

I began this exercise with apprehension, and I finish it with regrets. I find no
pleasure in it. Who, I ask myself, do you think you are to claim an entire interpretive tradition is in error? And, can this text stand up to similar levels of scrutiny?
To wit, I do not have good answers.

Yet, I find the discrepancies between the original texts and the interpretations
irreconcilable. Initially I assumed I was wrong, that I just didn't get it, that
I was missing an essential hermeneutic key. The deeper I dug, however, the more I
found myself mired in the interpretive chasm—and the more convinced I became
that the missing hermeneutic key was endemic to the communication field, and a
reflection of its isolation from interdisciplinary discourse.

The Lippmann of communication is not the Lippmann of sociology, history,
or philosophy, although a few scholars such as Clifford Christians, Daniel Hallin,
Hanno Hardt, Michael Schudson, and Peter Simonson, who contribute to the
communication literature, have more expansive and appreciative understandings
of Lippmann's work.[127] The young Lippmann's identity as a Jamesian pragmatist
tempered by Santayana's naturalism and his own experiential learning is well established in other disciplinary conventions. Increasingly Lippmann is being reread as
anticipating postmodernism and struggling, as we struggle, to resolve its contra-
dictions: John Patrick Diggins, for example, claims that "Lippmann foresaw the
postmodernist implications of pragmatism a half-century before Richard Rorty
and Jürgen Habermas returned to American philosophy to develop new ways of
thinking about politics and society that required no metaphysical foundations."[128]

Once I located these broader interpretive streams, I knew there was no turning back. Having longstanding commitments to exposing constitutive censorships,

I had to plead Lippmann's case: not to advocate for his views per se, but for a fair hearing for them in communication—the field he speaks to most directly in the time period that we have been considering.

If there are lessons to learn from this exercise, they are remarkably prosaic in a post-Derrida interpretive era:

- History matters. When history is neglected, the void is filled by information that was not intended to carry its weight.
- Secondary sources should supplement, not displace, primary sources.
- Understanding the context—historical, social, and economic conditions—of cultural production is imperative. Although they can never fully succeed, scholars must try to see the world and especially the future as their historical subjects saw them.
- No subject or historical figure has been "done"; every generation needs to reread the classics in light of new problems and sensibilities.
- Disciplinary isolation provides fertile grounds for cultivating error.
- Beware of dichotomies: human thought and the social worlds in which it takes form are complex, paradoxical.
- Beware of methodolatry: approaches to research that value method more than substance. Yet, putting method, broadly conceived, before political ideology, a praxis modeled by Lippmann, is not necessarily the post-Foucaultian anachronism it might initially seem. To be sure, there are no ideologically uncontaminated methods in the social sciences or humanities, but methodical, critically reflexive, disciplined thought—Lippmann's ascetic of disinterestedness—can still help us to expand the pictures in our own heads.
- Take Lippmann's advice. Recognize that human knowledge is limited, and that humility is not only prudent, but also wise.
- Exercise extreme caution in equating analysis with agency.

The last point requires elaboration. The relationship between authors and agency is thorny. As the root suggests, to be an author is to claim authority and exercise agency. This raises the question of responsibility: when we release ideas into the world, what responsibility do we have for what others make of them?

Is Lippmann responsible for Lasswell and Bernays? Goebbels reportedly read Bernays. Is Bernays responsible for Goebbels? Is Lippmann? What are Machiavelli's responsibilities? Is Marx responsible for Stalin? Or dialectically, is Stalin responsible for Glasnost? Chains of interpretation and influence invert, multiple, and fracture.

Jacques Ellul vowed not to write any more about propaganda because he became aware that readers could read against the intent of his opus, *Propaganda:*

The Formation of Men's Attitudes (1973). Is it better to remain silent, to self-censor, than to identify and challenge perversions of power because an aspiring tyrant might twist critique into advocacy?[129]

Lippmann has been compared to Max Weber, and there are indeed some remarkable parallels in the thought and careers of the two men. Weber thought it was the duty of the teacher to confront students with inconvenient facts.[130] Lippmann, the cosmopolitan critic of all concentrations of power, thought it was his duty as a political columnist and public intellectual to confront readers with inconvenient ideas: to probe the underside of the dialectic—Leibling's "on-the one-hand-this-writer." Weber described the "iron cage" of modernity as well as the dangers posed by the irrational appeal of charismatic leadership, the rise of "new Caesars."[131] Yet, to my knowledge, Weber has not been blamed for the harsh realities of modern life or the rise of Hitler. Rather, he is praised for his prescience and sociological acumen. In contrast, as we have seen, some scholars implicate Lippmann in the collapse of the public sphere. Should they?

There are no definitive answers to these questions. John Peters explores this conundrum in *Courting the Abyss* (2005). He comes down on the side of publication, but reserves the right of a Pauline shudder in the face of evil.[132] Perhaps that is the best we can do. I shudder at what Goebbels made of Bernays.

As survivors of postmodernism, we know that texts are fluid, signifiers float, and arguments implode; however, once again I invoke the prosaic, and plead for what I will call the hermeneutic golden rule: read others as you would have them read you. Mistakes happen: critique is their corrective. Save the shudders for the hard cases: lies and willful inversions. Yes, I am aware of the deep irony of this invocation in the context of the present chapter: for I have read others' work harshly although, by my lights, with integrity. To wit, I remind the reader of my introductory caveat: I do not discard the baby with the metaphoric bath water. My critique is not a wholesale indictment of the work of the authors examined here: it is very narrowly directed to their interpretations of Lippmann.

Finally, since the appearance of Ronald Steel's biography of Lippmann, dumping on Lippmann has become fashionable, especially among journalists, who are eager to discard the professional cant about journalistic objectivity that they acquired in "j-school." Many recognize that it is fraudulent, and believe Lippmann perpetrated the fraud.[133] As we have seen, that is not so.

Lippmann was, to be sure, often wrong, as he readily admitted; and all rereadings of his work must be insistently critical. Nevertheless, as Roy Porter reminds us, the purpose of history is not to "paint pictures of forward-looking 'heroes' slaying reactionary tyrants and bigots to create a better future." Such "saints and sinners" histories, he warns, "nowadays themselves appear partisan and prejudiced."[134] Warts-and-all histories are far more prudent. Yet, I yield to the temptation to counterbalance Carey's honorifics, which celebrate Dewey as a twentieth-century hero "for a lifetime of courageous intellectual and public service," by suggesting that Lippmann—although no hero—also lived such a life. It required intellectual courage to criticize the Creel Commission during and after World War I, expose the *New York Times'* ideologically laden coverage of the Russian Revolution, oppose the Palmer Raids and the Red Scare, criticize Franklin Roosevelt's court-packing, refuse to see Russia through the binary lens of the cold war, denounce McCarthyism, contest America's imperial adventures in Latin America, criticize the CIA, support publication of the Pentagon Papers, and oppose the Vietnam War. There were warts too. My own reservations about Lippmann's work are extensive. As we have seen, however, views which he explicitly rejected have been imputed to him; and he has been excoriated for them.

Within current journalistic lore, the courage of broadcast journalists Edward R. Murrow and Walter Cronkite is widely recognized: Murrow for taking on McCarthyism on his CBS program *See It Now*, on March 9, 1954, and Cronkite for reversing his support for the Vietnam War in his "We are mired in a stalemate" editorial on CBS News on February 27, 1968. Walter Lippmann opposed McCarthy right from the beginning, and was repeatedly red-baited and slandered for it. Lippmann was also an early and insistent critic of the Vietnam War; his criticism influenced "insiders" such as Senators Church and Fulbright, and Undersecretary of State George Ball. His opposition to the war cost Lippmann many longtime friends and his dubious status as a Washington insider. Lyndon Johnson was so furious with Lippmann that he launched a systematic campaign to discredit him, and could not resist taking a parting shot at him in his Farewell Address. In sum, Lippmann paid a much higher price than Murrow or Cronkite for his journalistic courage, and he has not yet been reimbursed by posterity.

NOTES

1. Toulmin, *Cosmopolis*, 13.
2. Mander, *Communication in Transition;* and Hardt, *Critical Communication Studies*. Mander points out that all communication is mediated, dependent upon historical context. To ignore history is therefore a fundamental, constitutive, error in the conception of communication research. Hardt offers a comprehensive analysis of the consequences for communication research of the neglect of history.
3. Anderson, *Imagined Communities*. The processes of legitimating academic disciplines and nation-states are similar in many ways. More than most academic fields, communication has contested boundaries and internal fractures. Misinterpretations of Lippmann's work are widespread within the field but take different forms in journalism, effects research, propaganda studies, and the cultural critique of effects research. Not every communication researcher subscribes to the dominant view; however, it is deeply enough ingrained in the field as to constitute something approaching an orthodox view.

4. Google Book Search and Google Scholar make it possible to track the frequency of citations as well as patterns of influence by pairing names in the search engines. For example, pairing Walter Lippmann and James Carey identifies all books in the database in which third authors refer to both men as well as the page numbers of these references. The text of the joint citations can then be accessed to determine whether an author is basing claims about Lippmann's work on a primary source, a secondary source, or both. In addition, third and even fourth degrees of separation can be identified, when for example, an author relies on and acknowledges Carey's interpretive influence, as Jay Rosen does, but then others build upon Carey's interpretation without acknowledging it; this can be done by comparing frequencies of references to Rosen and Lippmann to references to Rosen, Carey, and Lippmann. Scholars presumably display biases in favor of citing more recent sources, especially in the case of secondary sources (Ewen rather than Schramm); to cite more prominent scholars (Chomsky rather than Jansen); and those with name recognition in their own discipline (in communication, Carey or Schramm rather than Blum or Riccio).

5. Dillon, "Present Tense, Past Tense."

6. Reston, "The Mockingbird and the Taxicab," 226–38.

7. Lippmann, "William James," 20–23. The original appeared in *Everybody's Magazine*, edited by Lincoln Steffens in 1910. This kind of radical openness to and rigorous interrogation of evidence would later be named, formalized, elevated to methodological status, and advocated by phenomenologists as "surrender and catch." See Wolff, *Survival and Sociology*.

8. There have been numerous biographies of Lippmann: none more comprehensive than Steel's, *Walter Lippmann and the American Century*. Yet, even Steel, a journalist, glosses over the significance of Lippmann's more scholarly endeavors in favor of a focus on his writings on international affairs, interactions with famous people, and his personal life. Consequently, Steel misses the significance of cosmopolitanism as the recurrent theme of Lippmann's thought—a lapse that Blum corrects in *Walter Lippmann*.

9. John Dewey may have been the only contemporary who fully appreciated Lippmann's epistemological achievement. See Dewey's review of *Public Opinion*. For assessments of it in light of the postmodern crisis of knowledge, see Diggins, *The Promise of Pragmatism*; Riccio, *Walter Lippmann*; and Graebner, *The Engineering of Consent*.

10. Lerner, *Ideas are Weapons*, 191; Halberstam, *The Powers that Be*, 368; and Steel, *Walter Lippmann*, xvii.

11. Schlesinger, "Walter Lippmann: The Intellectual v. Politics," 189–225. Luskin interprets Schlesinger's view of Lippmann in very similar terms. See Luskin, *Lippmann, Liberty, and the Press*.

12. Lippmann's view of science was influenced by C. S. Peirce. Lippmann's early critique of scientific arrogance and reductionism is found in *Drift and Mastery*.

13. A. J. Liebling quoted by Luskin, *Lippmann, Liberty, and the Press*, 154.

14. Blum, *Walter Lippmann*, 16.

15. Halberstam, *The Powers that Be*. Riccio argues that Lippmann put method before doctrine: that was the whole point of his attempt to develop a politics of "disinterestedness." Lippmann linked ideological purity to censorship: "Clear doctrine and rigid purposes that apply to a whole nation have to be paid for; their price is the suppression of individuality and the regimentation of opinion" (Lippmann quoted in Riccio, *Walter Lippmann*, 105)."

16. Lippmann, *Public Opinion*, 168.

17. Lippmann distinguished between his method as a political columnist, where he issued opinions three times a week in *Today and Tomorrow*, and his more scholarly works. He described the columns as "sketches in the sand that the sea will wash away." Yet, he recognized that lasting knowledge requires withdrawal from the pressing issues of the moment so that scholars can

"collaborate with their ancestors." He maintained that the true scholar, unlike the editorial writer, is "always radical," "preoccupied with presumptions, with antecedents, and probabilities . . . in a world where choices are more numerous and possibilities more varied than they are at the level of practical decisions." For the scholar, unlike the journalist, the present, the "sketch in the sand," is a "mere fragment of the past." Endorsing the value of systematic methods in producing reliable knowledge, he admitted that his journalism lacked that kind of discipline. He saw the work of the journalist as involving essentially the same responsibility that democracy imposes on every sovereign citizen, except that the correspondent has the advantages of time and proximity: "In some field of interest, we make it our business to find out what is going on under the surface and beyond the horizon, to infer, to deduce, to imagine, and to guess what is going on inside, what this meant yesterday, and what it could mean tomorrow." He also acknowledges, even exaggerates, the limits of this approach: "whatever truth you contribute to the world will be one lucky shot in a thousand misses" (Lippmann, "A Declaration of Faith and Hope," 534–38, originally published in 1963 and from which the above quotations are excerpted, and Lippmann, "The Scholar in a Troubled World," 509–15. Originally published 1963 and 1932)."

18. Paul Roazen contends that Lippmann's reputation is now "under a cloud," and makes the case that Steel bears considerable responsibility for this. Acknowledging that there is often some eclipse in public reputation after death, he nevertheless argues that Steel's "dislike of his subject" is palpable. My own interpretation of Steel is that he was certainly ambivalent about his subject: sometimes quite empathetic, even indulgent, but at others times he seems impatient with Lippmann's decisions and views. Some of this may simply be biographer's pique; for example, one is attracted to a mythic figure and finds a fallible human; sheer exhaustion may also be a factor, given the enormity of Steel's undertaking and the complexity of Lippmann as subject. Moreover, Lippmann was highly ambivalent about being the subject of an authorized biography, preferring to focus on the present and future, instead of the past. Richard H. Rovere, who was initially selected as the authorized biographer but eventually turned the project over to Steel, describes the problems that Lippmann's ambivalence posed in "Walter Lippmann." All Lippmann scholars do nonetheless owe Steel an enormous debt for his thorough and meticulous chronological coverage of Lippmann's long and complex life, and for his thoughtful attempts to contextualize historically Lippmann's political thought. In support of Roazen's view, however, Steel broke his agreement with Lippmann not to write about anything "personal"—an inexplicable bargain for a biographer—probing deeply into his personal life and publishing excerpts of Lippmann's love letters to his second wife (with her permission), which the intensely private Lippmann would have never consented to. One does come away from the book feeling the taint of voyeurism. Lippmann was of advanced age and in poor health when Steel conducted his interviews with him, yet Steel is critical of inconsistencies in Lippmann's memory of his past views and the written record of them. Steel, a young man when he wrote the book, is not as sensitive to the nature of the aging memory as some of us may wish. For a wonderful autobiographical account of the phenomenon Steel was witnessing but unable to comprehend, see Eric Hobsbawm's autobiography in which he explores the discrepancies among his current memory of past events, accounts he wrote at the time of the event, and the current consensus view of historians about the event: it should be required reading for all biographers of aged subjects. (Steel, *Walter Lippmann* and Roazen, *Encountering Freud*, 285–86; and Hobsbawm, *Interesting Times*.)

19. Blum, *Walter Lippmann;* and Riccio, *Walter Lippmann*.

20. Blum, *Walter Lippmann;* and Rossiter and Lare, *The Essential Lippmann*.

21. Peterson, "The Press as a Social Institution," 90.

22. Blum, *Walter Lippmann*, 14.

23. Wallas, a British Fabian socialist on a year's leave at Harvard, was Lippmann's teacher. When Wallas published *The Great Society*, he dedicated it to Lippmann. (Wallas, *The Great Society*.)

24. Hollinger, "Ethnic Diversity," 133–51. Blum also cites Hollinger. Hollinger credits Bourne with the original articulation of cosmopolitanism in his 1916 article, "Trans-National America." The idea does, however, have much older roots in Pierre Bayle's *Republic of Letters*, Oliver Goldsmith's *Citizens of the World*, and the encyclopedia movements of the eighteenth century, and in America, in the work of Whitman and James (Jansen, *Censorship*)." Cosmopolitanism is also in fashion again today as a philosophical response to globalization. For advocacy and critique, see Nussbaum, *For Love of Country*.

25. Hollinger, "Ethnic Diversity," 140.

26. Ibid. Hollinger acknowledges that cosmopolitanism resonates with the anti-Semitic stereotype of the rootless Jew; to a considerable extend, it inverted the sign from negative to positive and expanded the metaphor of the journey to include all scholars open to the modern (secular) quest for a new intellectual and aesthetic sensibility.

27. Coles examines this aesthetic in *Doing Documentary Work*.

28. Blum, *Walter Lippmann*.

29. Riccio, *Walter Lippmann*, 127.

30. Lasch, *The New Radicalism;* and Lippmann, *American Inquisitors*. Dewey's defense of Lippmann appears in his review of *The Phantom Public*. Sociologist Graham Wallas, a disillusioned Fabian socialist, exercised strong influence over his student; moreover, he introduced young Lippmann to prominent members of the Fabian group, including H.G. Wells, George Bernard Shaw, and Beatrice and Sidney Webb. With Lippmann, the elitism of the Fabian influence was tempered by the democratic values of James, Dewey, Jane Addams, Thorstein Veblen, and others. The literature on crowd psychology, prominent in the late nineteenth century, was another strain of elitist thought that exercised a general influence on Progressive thought and its preoccupation with social order. Lippmann was also conversant in American and European social science of his day. Steel provides a balanced account of these influences in *Walter Lippmann and the American Century*. Conversely, it should be pointed out that, despite his cosmopolitanism, Lippmann worked consciously to develop a style that was accessible to the "robust middle" of American literacy. This was not simply a market-driven decision, but part of a principled movement involving Lippmann, Van Wyck Brooks, Randolph Bourne, and others to emulate Walt Whitman by avoiding "highbrow" academic language and addressing the average, interested citizen. (Lippmann, 1914 letter to Brooks, quoted by Steven Biel, *Independent Intellectuals in the United States, 1910–1945*.) Brooks articulated this democratic intellectual credo in "Highbrow and Lowbrow."

31. Luskin, *Lippmann, Liberty, and the Press*, 238.

32. Lippmann, *Liberty and the News*, 44.

33. Halberstam, *The Powers that Be*, 372.

34. Haskell, *Objectivity is Not Neutrality*, 84.

35. Ibid., 92.

36. Ibid. Wilfred M. McClay offers excellent exegeses of the heavy semantic loads Progressives attached to the terms interests and disinterestedness in his introduction to the Transaction edition of *The Phantom Public*.

37. In this regard, he was enacting the values of James, which he applauded in "William James." The ascetic ethic that Lippmann recommended to scholars was common among scientists attempting to identify and root out bias in the nineteenth and early twentieth century. See Daston and Galison, "The Image of Objectivity." Lippmann's version of ascetic method resonates with the values embraced by Weber in "Science as a Vocation."

38. Luskin, *Lippmann, Liberty, and the Press*, 58.

39. I make this claim about *Liberty and the News* with full confidence only because a fully searchable edition is available online. (Tuchman, "Objectivity as Strategic Ritual.")

40. Lippmann, "Two Revolutions in the American Press;" and Schiller, *Objectivity and the News*.

41. Lippmann, "Two Revolutions in the American Press."

42. Ibid., 439.

43 Ibid., 440.

44. Lippmann, *Public Opinion;* and Lippmann, "Two Revolutions in the American Press," 441.

45. The lineage connecting Lippmann to critical realism is direct via Santayana's naturalism. Lippmann always acknowledged his philosophical debt to Santayana, and saw realism as a counter to the relativism of James's pragmatism. For articulations of contemporary forms of critical realism, see Baskar, *A Realist Theory of Science;* and for a comprehensive bibliography, see "Critical Realism (WSCR)," accessed September 22, 2006, at www.raggedclaws.com/criticalrealism/.

46. Lippmann, *Public Opinion*, 226.

47. Riccio, *Walter Lippmann*, 164.

48. Lippmann, *Public Opinion*, 226.

49. Ibid., 226.

50. Ibid., 227.

51. Lippmann refers to "social facts" here in Durkheim's sense of the term. Although he does not cite Durkheim here, elsewhere Lippmann does demonstrate familiarity with European sociology of the period.

52. Lippmann, *Public Opinion*, 229.

53. Lippmann, "Two Revolutions in the American Press," 439; and Lippmann, *Public Opinion*, 228.

54. By intelligence bureaus, Lippmann meant independent (of political and commercial "interests") record-keeping and knowledge-producing organizations. In addition to university research and independent research institutes, this included government agencies like the Bureau of Standards or, to use a current example, the General Accounting Office, which audits government spending for waste and fraud. He was not literally advocating creation of government surveillance or the CIA, as Glander seems to imply in linking Lippmann's idea to William Langer, founder and first director of the CIA's Office of National Estimates and his 1947 plan for developing the CIA. Lippmann frequently expressed concerns about the trade-offs of liberty for national security that the U.S. made during the cold war; and he was a critic of the CIA. (Glander, *Origins of Mass Communication Research*, 62.)

55. Lippmann, *Liberty and the News*, 66.

56. Diggins, *The Promise of Pragmatism*. Hoopes argues, however, that Lippmann misunderstood Peirce, a misunderstanding that he inherited from William James's misinterpretation of Peirce's logical communitarianism. (Hoopes, *Community Denied*.)

57. Schudson, *Discovering the News*.

58. Carey, *Communication as Culture*, 75.

59. Lippmann's chapter was included in Schramm's 1949 volume, *Mass Communications*, absent from his 1954 edition of *The Process and Effects of Mass Communication*, and included in the 1971 revision of *The Process and Effects of Mass Communication* (co-edited with Donald F. Roberts). Lippmann's absence from the 1954 volume is telling. Instead of Lippmann, who invented the concept of "stereotype," there is a chapter on "National Stereotypes" by William Buchanan and Hadley Cantril. The 1954 edition of *The Process and Effects of Mass Communication* was originally produced as a training manual for the U.S. Information Agency. Lippmann opposed the establishment of a permanent U.S. propaganda agency and called for the elimination of the

Voice of America after World War II. (Schramm, *Mass Communications*; Schramm, *The Process and Effects of Mass Communications;* and Schramm and Roberts, *The Process and Effects of Mass Communications.*)

60. Schramm, *The Beginnings of Communication Study in America.*

61. Simpson documents Lazarsfeld's praise as well as Lasswell's Machiavellian inversion. Hardt also recognizes Lippmann's influence on Lasswell. (Simpson, *Science of Coercion*; and Hardt, *Critical Communication Studies.*)

62. Bryant and Zillman, *Media Effects.* As of September 12, 2006; Google Book Search yields 80,100 pages for agenda setting and Google Scholar yields 295,000 citations; this is, of course, a very crude indicator of influence since the large numbers preclude sorting for relevance.

63. Ibid. McCombs and Estrada describe agenda-setting as "Lippmann's intellectual offspring" in "The News and the Pictures in Our Head."

64. Glasser contends that Lippmann "detailed the gatekeeper tradition." (Glasser, *Public Opinion,* 296.)

65. Lippmann, *Public Opinion,* 97. Stereotype was a technical term used in printing. Lippmann's innovation was to expand its meaning and apply it to social cognition.

66. Allport, *The Nature of Prejudice;* and Glick, Rudman, and Dovodio, *The Nature of Prejudice.*

67. Lippmann, *Public Opinion,* 143; and Lazarsfeld and Katz, *Personal Influence,* xxxi.

68. Gerbner, "Toward a General Model of Communication."

69. Hardt has revived interest in Lippmann and Merz's "A Test of the News" (a supplement to the *New Republic* August 4, 1920) by arguing that the study is a founding work in international communications. (Hardt, "Reading the Russian Revolution.")

70. Bernays, *Propaganda.*

71. Bernays, *Crystallizing Public Opinion.*

72. Lippmann, *Liberty and the Press,* 8.

73. Bernays, *Crystallizing Public Opinion,* 122.

74. Lippmann, *Public Opinion,* 218.

75. Ibid. Boorstin extended Lippmann's idea to describe pseudo-events in *The Image.*

76. Lasswell, *Propaganda Technique,* 6.

77. Simpson, *Science of Coercion,* 77.

78. Lasswell, *Propaganda Technique,* 12.

79. Lippmann, "Two Revolutions in the American Press," 439.

80. Steel, *Walter Lippmann,* 143.

81. Ibid.

82. Ibid.

83. Ibid., 143–47.

84. Lippmann, "William James," 23; Wiebe, *The Search for Order*; Lasch, *The New Radicalism*; and Forcey, *The Crossroads of Liberalism.* Much of course depends on how one defines propaganda. While I recognize that all attempts to do so are contestable, here I follow the precedent of Jowett and O'Donnell who distinguish between propaganda and persuasion in *Propaganda and Persuasion.*

85. Dewey's father served in the Union Army. This background factor is not given much attention, yet Justice Oliver Wendell Holmes, who was a significant personal influence on the young Lippmann, was a wounded veteran of the war, and was known for his war stories as well as his realism and skepticism, which are usually attributed to his war experience.

86. Lippmann, quoted in Riccio, *Walter Lippmann,* 170–71. Orig. text in Lippmann, *The Good Society.*

87. Chomsky, *Media Control,* 10

88. Ibid., 12–13.

89. Pairing of Chomsky and Lippmann in Google Book Search yields 364 matches.

90. Ewen, *PR!*, 9.

91. Ibid., 159.

92. Ibid., 152.

93. Ibid., 155.

94. Ibid., 154.

95. Ibid., 158.

96. Ibid., 158.

97. Ibid., 152.

98. Ibid., 154 and 153.

99. Ibid., 153. Despite Ewen's framing of Lippmann's brief references to film as exceptional and therefore "prescriptive," the new media had in fact attracted significant social commentary long before 1922. Daniel J. Czitrom provides a concise history of the reception of the new media of film by American thinkers and reformers in the first two decades of the twentieth century. (See Czitrom, *Media and the American Mind*.)

100. Toulmin, *Cosmopolis*, 1.

101. Lippmann, *Public Opinion*, 158.

102. Ibid., 256.

103. In his most recent book *Typecasting* (a collaboration with Elizabeth Ewen), the "clairvoyant" Lippmann is foregrounded as anticipating typecasting with the concept of stereotyping; curiously, there is no residue of the highly critical earlier assessment of Lippmann.

104. Lippmann, *Early Writings*. Some studies of pragmatism suggest that young Lippmann's version of pragmatism was more faithful to James's than Dewey's. Richard M. Gale maintains that throughout his life Dewey distorted interpretation of James's philosophy to position himself as its direct heir. (Gale, "William James and John Dewey.") Hoopes argues that Lippmann's pragmatism was in error because it was so dependent on what Hoopes regards as James's "weak" version of pragmatism. (Hoopes, *Community Denied*.)

105. Simonson, "Pragmatism and Communication."

106. Carey, *Communication as Culture*, 79.

107. Carey, "The Press and Public Discourse" and Carey, "Commentary: Communication and the Progressives"; Carey, "The Press, Public Opinion, and Public Discourse"; and Carey, "The Chicago School."

108. Carey, "The Chicago School," 23. Even Dewey's biographer Robert B. Westbrook does not claim that Dewey was ever able successfully to counter Lippmann's democratic realism. (Westbrook, *John Dewey and American Democracy*.)

109. Carey, "Recovering 'Mass' and 'Media.'"

110. Carey, *Communication as Culture*, 97.

111. Carey, "Commentary: Communication and the Progressives," 265. Faithful to the legacy of his hero, Carey embraces a form of Deweyan strategic utopianism whereby one imagines and valorizes idealized versions of social reality in hope of bringing them to fruition. Dewey, for example, promoted community based face-to-face conversations on the assumption that democracy would be realized in the communications themselves although he did not explain how these communications, if successful, could transform the body politic. Carey saw "nostalgia for what never was"—a vibrant fully democratic public sphere—as a useful fiction ("desire") that might lead to its realization. Salutary visions of the future may indeed be useful in mobilizing social movements. In advocating them, however, we are doing normative philosophy or politics; not describing what is (or was). The past may inspire such fictions, but inspiration and fiction (useful

or not) are governed by different norms of truth telling than the canons or rhetoric of history, regardless of the plurality, fallibility, and contestability of the latter. Looking backward rather than forward through the lens of the "ritual" approach to communication, may therefore be hazardous to descriptive truth. Lippmann, his relationships to James, Dewey, and his pragmatism may be casualties of this approach. On Dewey, see Goodman, "Democracy and Public Discussion" and Carey, "Public Sphere." I am indebted to Jefferson Pooley for the provocation that produced this note although not necessarily its conclusions.

112. Carey, *Communication as Culture*, 78.

113. Carey, "Commentary: Communication and the Progressives," 271.

114. Ibid., 268.

115. Ibid., 281.

116. Christopher Lasch criticizes Dewey on exactly these grounds, however, claiming that equating school and life is fallacious. In Lasch's view, the classroom, unlike life, is where social control and planning are most easily imposed. The "freedom" cultivated in the classroom is embedded within an authoritarian structure. Lasch argues that the school ought to be at a significant remove from life (politics). (Lasch, *The New Radicalism in America*.)

117. J. S. Mill quoted by Lippmann, *Liberty and the News*, 32.

118. Lippmann, *The Good Society*; and Lippmann, *The Public Philosophy*.

119. Carey, "The Press, Public Opinion, and Public Discourse," 246.

120. Google Scholar yields the most interesting results here. As of September 12, 2006, entries using three names, John Durham Peters, James W. Carey, Walter Lippmann, yielded 41 hits, while entries for John Durham Peters and Walter Lippmann yielded 114 hits. The triad of Jay Rosen, James W. Carey, and Walter Lippmann yielded 54 hits, while Jay Rosen and Walter Lippmann yielded 163. Although Peters and Rosen do take their own efforts beyond Carey's initial for-mulation, and cite Lippmann in contexts unrelated to Carey's interpretation, the pattern does nevertheless suggest, at least crudely, that at the third level of interpretation, evidence of the original source recedes, as it becomes shared knowledge: the disciplinary view.

121. Peters, "Democracy and American Mass Communication Theory."

122. For Peters's revised views, see Peters, "Why Dewey Wasn't So Right and Lippmann Wasn't So Wrong"; Peters, *Speaking into the Air*; Peters, "Public Journalism and Democratic Theory"; and Peters, "Sinfulness, Saintliness, and Monkey Business." For a recent effort that builds upon Carey and Peters's earlier view, see Soderlund, "Rethinking a Curricular Icon." Soderlund's work is admirable in the sense that she does go to the original sources, the work of Lippmann and his contemporaries, but she still sees Lippmann through the inherited interpretive legacy of the communication field. In that sense, her essay adds to the field's preferred reading instead of "rethinking" it.

123. Peters offers the Plato and Aristotle categorization in "Historical Tensions."

124. Peters, "Democracy and American Mass Communication Theory," 207.

125. For Carey's critical response, see Carey, "Commentary: Communication and the Progressives." Conversely, Carey provides an enthusiastic blurb for the cover of Peters's *Speaking into the Air*.

126. Jay Rosen, *What Are Journalist For?* For a personal account of Carey influence on his thinking, see Rosen, "Introduction/ 'We'll Have That Conversation.'"

127. Christians, Ferre, and Fackler, *Good News*; Hallin, *The "Uncensored War"*; Hardt, "Reading the Russian Revolution"; Schudson, *Discovering the News*; Schudson, "The Public Journalism Movement" and Simonson, "Pragmatism and Communication."

128. Diggins, "From Pragmatism to Natural Law"; and Diggins, *The Promise of Pragmatism*. See also Riccio, *Walter Lippmann*; and Graebner, *The Engineering of Consent*.

129. I thank Lee Artz for reminding me of this.
130. Weber, "Science as a Vocation;" and Weber, *The Protestant Ethic and the Spirit of Capitalism.*
131. Weber, "Politics as a Vocation."
132. Peters, *Courting the Abyss.*
133. Lippmann reportedly was ranked a lowly sixty-fourth in a recent list of the all-time great journalists. (MacPherson, *All Governments Lie!*)
134. Porter, *The Enlightenment*, 1.

WORKS CITED

Allport, Gordon. *The Nature of Prejudice.* New York: Doubleday Anchor, 1958.
Anderson, Benedict. *Imagined Communities: Reflections on the Origins and Spread of Nationalism.* London: Verso, 1981.
Baskar, Roy. *A Realist Theory of Science.* London: Verso, 1997.
Bernays, Edward L. *Crystallizing Public Opinion.* New York: Boni and Liveright, 1923.
———. *Propaganda.* New York: Horace Liveright, 1928.
Biel, Steven. *Independent Intellectuals in the United States, 1910–1945.* New York: New York University Press, 1992.
Blum, D. Steven. *Walter Lippmann: Cosmopolitanism in the Century of Total War.* Ithaca, NY: Cornell University Press, 1984.
Boorstin, Daniel. *The Image: A Guide to Pseudo-events.* New York: Vintage, 1992.
Brooks, Van Wyck. "Highbrow and Lowbrow." *Forum* LIII, no. 4 (April 1915): 337–41.
Bryant, Jennings, and Dolf Zillman. *Media Effects: Advances in Theory and Research.* Mahwah, NJ: Lawrence Erlbaum, 2002.
Carey, James W. "The Chicago School and the History of Mass Communication Research." In *James Carey: A Critical Reader,* edited by Eve Stryker Munson and Catherine A. Warren, 14–33. Minneapolis: University of Minnesota Press, 1997.
———. "Commentary: Communication and the Progressives." *Critical Studies in Mass Communication* 6 (1989): 264–282.
———. *Communication as Culture: Essays on Media and Society.* Boston: Unwin Hyman, 1989.
———. "The Press and Public Discourse." *Center Magazine* 20, no. 2 (1987): 4–32.
———. "The Press, Public Opinion, and Public Discourse: On the Edge of the Postmodern." In *James Carey: A Critical Reader,* edited by Eve Stryker Munson and Catherine A. Warren, 228–57. Minneapolis: University of Minnesota Press, 1997.
———. "Public Sphere," plenary address presented at the annual meeting of the International Communication Association, Chicago, IL, May 23, 1996.
Chomsky, Noam. *Media Control: The Spectacular Achievements of Propaganda.* New York: Seven Stories Press, 1997.
Christians, Clifford G., John P. Ferre, and P. Mark Fackler. *Good News: Social Ethics and the Press.* New York: Oxford University Press, 1993.
Coles, Robert. *Doing Documentary Work.* New York: Oxford University Press, 1997.
"Critical Realism (WSCR)." www.raggedclaws.com/criticalrealism/ (accessed September 22, 2006).
Curry Jansen, Sue. *Censorship: The Knot that Binds Power and Knowledge.* New York: Oxford University Press, 1988.
Czitrom, Daniel J. *Media and the American Mind: From Morse to McLuhan.* Chapel Hill: University of North Carolina Press, 1982.

Daston, Lorraine, and Peter Galison. "The Image of Objectivity." *Representations* 40 (Autumn 1992): 81–128.

Dewey, John. Review of *The Phantom Public*, by Walter Lippmann. *New Republic* 45 (December 2, 1925): 52–54.

———. Review of *Public Opinion*, by Walter Lippmann. *New Republic* 30 (May 3, 1922): 286–88.

Diggins, John P. "From Pragmatism to Natural Law: Walter Lippmann's Quest for the Foundations of Legitimacy," *Political Theory* 19, no.4 (November 1991): 535.

———. *The Promise of Pragmatism: Modernism and the Crisis of Knowledge and Authority.* Chicago: University of Chicago Press, 1994.

Dillon, Mike. "Present Tense, Past Tense: The Historical Roots of Civic Journalism." Pew Center. www.pewcenter.org/doingcj/speeches/a_dillon.shtml (accessed September 22, 2006).

Ewen, Stuart. *PR!: A Social History of Spin.* New York: Basic Books, 1996.

Ewen, Stuart, and Elizabeth Ewen. *Typecasting: On the Arts and Sciences of Human Inequality.* New York: Seven Stories Press, 2006.

Forcey, Charles. *The Crossroads of Liberalism: Croly, Weyl, Lippmann, and the Progressive Era 1900–1925.* Oxford: Oxford University Press, 1961.

Gale, Richard M. "William James and John Dewey: The Odd Couple." *Midwest Journal of Philosophy* 28, no. 1 (2004): 149–67.

Gerbner, George. "Toward a General Model of Communication." In *Gerbner, Against the Mainstream: The Selected Works of George Gerbner*, edited by Michael Morgan, 37–60. New York: Peter Lang, 2002.

Glander, Timothy. *Origins of Mass Communication Research During the Cold War: Educational Efforts and Contemporary Implications.* Mahwah, NJ: Lawrence Erlbaum, 2000.

Glasser, Theodore L. *Public Opinion and the Communication of Consent.* New York: Guilford, 1995.

Glick, Peter, Laurie A. Rudman, and John F. Dovodio. *The Nature of Prejudice: Fifty Years After Allport.* Oxford: Blackwell, 2005.

Goodman, David. "Democracy and Public Discussion in the Progressive and New Deal Eras." *Studies in American Political Development* 18 (2004): 81–111.

Graebner, William. *The Engineering of Consent: Democracy and Authority in Twentieth Century America.* Madison, WI: University of Wisconsin Press, 1987.

Halberstam, David. *The Powers that Be.* New York: Alfred A. Knopf, 1979.

Hallin, Daniel C. *The 'Uncensored War': The Media and Vietnam.* New York: Oxford University Press, 1989.

Hardt, Hanno. *Critical Communication Studies: Communication, History and Theory in America.* London: Routledge, 1992.

———. "Reading the Russian Revolution: International Communication Research and the Journalism of Lippmann and Merz." *Mass Communication and Society* 5, no. 1 (Winter 2002): 25–39.

Haskell, Thomas. *Objectivity is Not Neutrality: Explanatory Schemes in History.* Baltimore: Johns Hopkins University Press, 1998.

Hobsbawm, Eric. *Interesting Times: A Twentieth Century Life.* New York: Vintage, 1996.

Hollinger, David A. "Ethnic Diversity, Cosmopolitanism and the Emergence of the American Liberal Intelligentsia." *American Quarterly* 27 (May 1975): 133–51.

———. "Trans-National America." *Atlantic* 118 (1916): 86–97.

Hoopes, James. *Community Denied: The Wrong Turn of Pragmatic Liberalism.* Ithaca, NY: Cornell University Press, 1998.

Jowett, Garth S., and Victoria O'Donnell. *Propaganda and Persuasion 4th ed.* Thousand Oaks, CA: Sage, 2006.

Katz, Elihu, and Paul F. Lazarsfeld, *Personal Influence: The Part Played by People in the Flow of Mass Communications.* Glencoe, IL: Free Press, 1955.

Lasch, Christopher. *The New Radicalism in America 1889–1963: The Intellectual as a Social Type*. New York: W.W. Norton, 1965.

Lasswell, Harold D. *Propaganda Technique in the World War*. New York: Peter Smith, 1938.

Lerner, Max. *Ideas are Weapons*. New York: Viking, 1939.

Lippmann, Walter. *American Inquisitors: A Commentary on Dayton and Chicago*. New York: Macmillan, 1928.

———. "A Declaration of Faith and Hope." In *The Essential Lippmann: A Political Philosophy for Liberal Democracy*, edited by Clinton Rossiter and James Lare, 534–38. New York: Random House, 1963.

———. *Drift and Mastery: An Attempt to Diagnose the Current Unrest*. Madison, WI: University of Wisconsin Press, 1985.

———. *Early Writings*. New York: Liveright, 1970.

———. *The Good Society*. New York: Grosset and Dunlap, 1936.

———. *Liberty and the News*. New Brunswick, NJ: Transaction, 1995.

———. *Phantom Public* with introduction Wilfred M. McClay. New Brunswick, NJ: Transaction, 1993.

———. *Public Opinion*. New York: Simon and Schuster, 1997.

———. *The Public Philosophy*. Boston: Little, Brown and Company, 1955.

———. "The Scholar in a Troubled World." In *The Essential Lippmann: A Political Philosophy for Liberal Democracy*, edited by Clinton Rossiter and James Lare, 509–15. New York: Random House, 1963.

———. "Two Revolutions in the American Press." *Yale Review* 20 (1931): 433–41.

———. "William James." In *Lippmann, Public Persons*, edited by Gilbert A. Harrison, 20–23. New York: Liveright, 1976.

Lippmann, Walter, and Charles Merz. "A Test of the News," a supplement to *the New Republic* (August 4, 1920).

Luskin, John. *Lippmann, Liberty, and the Press*. Alabama: University of Alabama Press, 1972.

MacPherson, Myra. *All Governments Lie! The Life and Times of Rebel Journalist I.F. Stone*. New York: Scribner, 2006.

Mander, Mary S. *Communication in Transition: Issues and Debates in Current Research*. New York: Praeger, 1983.

McCombs, Maxwell, and George Estrada. "The News and the Pictures in Our Head." In *Do Media Govern?* edited by Shanto Iyengar and Richard Reeves, 237–247. Thousand Oaks, CA: Sage, 1997.

Nussbaum, Martha C. *For Love of Country: A New Democracy Forum on the Limits of Patriotism*. Boston: Beacon Press, 1996.

Peters, John Durham. *Courting the Abyss: Free Speech and the Liberal Tradition*. Chicago: University of Chicago Press, 2005.

———. "Democracy and American Mass Communication Theory: Dewey, Lippmann, Lazarsfeld." *Communication* 11 (1989): 199–220.

———. "Historical Tensions in the Concept of Public Opinion." In *Public Opinion and the Communication of Consent*, edited by Theodore L. Glasser and Charles T. Salmon, 3–32. New York: Guilford, 1995.

———. "Public Journalism and Democratic Theory: Four Challenges." In *The Idea of Public Journalism*, edited by Theodore L. Glasser, 99–117. New York: Guilford, 1999.

———. "Sinfulness, Saintliness, and Monkey Business." *Social Science Research Council*. www.ssrc.org/programs/media/background/ (accessed on September 22, 2006).

———. *Speaking into the Air: A History of the Idea of Communication.* Chicago: University of Chicago Press, 1999.

———. "Why Dewey Wasn't So Right and Lippmann Wasn't So Wrong." Paper presented at the annual meeting of the International Communication Association, Montreal, 1997.

Peterson, Theodore. "The Press as a Social Institution." In *American Communication Research: The Remembered History,* edited by Everette Dennis and Ellen Wartella, 85–94. Mahwah, NJ: Lawrence Erlbaum, 1996.

Porter, Roy S. *The Enlightenment.* London: Palgrave Macmillan, 2001.

Reston, James. "The Mockingbird and the Taxicab." In *Walter Lippmann and His Times,* edited by Marquis Child and James Reston, 226–38. New York: Harcourt, Brace and Company, 1959.

Riccio, Barry D. *Walter Lippmann—Odyssey of a Liberal.* New Brunswick, NJ: Transaction Publishers, 1996.

Roazen, Paul. *Encountering Freud: The Politics and History of Psychoanalysis.* New Brunswick, NJ: Transaction Publishers, 2003.

Rosen, Jay. "Introduction/ 'We'll Have That Conversation': Journalism and Democracy in the Thought of James W. Carey." In *James Carey: A Critical Reader,* edited by Eve Stryker Munson and Catherine A. Warren, 191–206. Minneapolis: University of Minnesota Press, 1997.

———. *What Are Journalist For?* New Haven, CT: Yale University Press, 1999.

Rossiter, Clinton, and James Lare, eds. *The Essential Lippmann: A Political Philosophy for Liberal Democracy.* New York: Random House, 1963.

Rovere, Ronald H. "Walter Lippmann." *American Scholar* (Autumn 1975): 585–603.

Schiller, Daniel. *Objectivity and the News: The Public and the Rise of Commercial Journalism.* Philadelphia: University of Pennsylvania Press, 1981.

Schlesinger, Jr., Walter. "Walter Lippmann: The Intellectual v. Politics." In *Walter Lippmann and His Times,* edited by Marquis Child and James Reston, 189–225. New York: Harcourt, Brace and Company, 1959.

Schramm, Wilbur. *The Beginnings of Communication Study in America: A Personal Memoir,* edited by Steven Chaffee and Everette Rogers. Thousand Oaks, CA: Sage, 1997.

———, Ed. *Mass Communications.* Urbana: University of Illinois Press, 1949.

———, Ed. *The Process and Effects of Mass Communications.* Urbana: University of Illinois Press, 1954.

Schramm, Wilbur, and Donald F. Roberts, eds. *The Process and Effects of Mass Communications.* Urbana: University of Illinois Press, 1971.

Schudson, Michael. *Discovering the News.* New York: Basic Books, 1978.

———. "The Public Journalism Movement and Its Problems." In *The Politics of News, The News of Politics,* edited by Doris Graber, Denis McQuail, and Pippa Norris, 132–49. Washington, DC: Congressional Quarterly Press, 1998.

Simonson, Peter. "Pragmatism and Communication." In *American Pragmatism and Communication Research,* edited by David K. Perry, 1–26. Mahwah, NJ: Lawrence Erlbaum Associates, 2001.

Simpson, Christopher. *Science of Coercion: Communication Research and Psychological Warfare 1945–1960.* New York: Oxford University Press, 1994.

Soderlund, Gretchen. "Rethinking a Curricular Icon: The Institutional and Ideological Foundations of Walter Lippmann." *Communication Review* 8 (2005): 307–27.

Steel, Ronald. *Walter Lippmann and the American Century.* New Brunswick, NJ: Transaction Publishers, 1999.

Toulmin, Stephen. *Cosmopolis: The Hidden Agenda of Modernity.* Chicago: University of Chicago Press, 1990.

Tuchman, Gaye. "Objectivity as Strategic Ritual: An Examination of Newsmen's Notions of Objectivity," *American Journal of Sociology* 77, no. 4 (1972): 660–79.

Wallas, Graham. *The Great Society: A Psychological Analysis.* New York: Macmillan, 1917.

Weber, Max. "Politics as a Vocation." In *From Max Weber,* edited by H. H. Gerth and C. Wright Mills, 77–128. New York: Oxford University Press, 1946.

———. *The Protestant Ethic and the Spirit of Capitalism.* New York: Charles Scribner's Sons, 1958.

———. "Science as a Vocation." In *From Max Weber,* edited by H. H. Gerth and C. Wright Mills, 129–56. New York: Oxford University Press, 1946.

Westbrook, Robert B. *John Dewey and American Democracy.* Ithaca, NY: Cornell University Press, 1991.

Wiebe, Robert H. *The Search for Order: 1877–1920.* New York: Hill and Wang, 1967.

Wolff, Kurt H. *Survival and Sociology: Vindicating the Human Subject.* New Brunswick, NJ: Transaction Publishers, 1984.

CHAPTER FOUR

Feminist Historiography AND THE Field: Writing New Histories

LANA F. RAKOW

What is feminist history in the field of communication? Is it a history of women in the field? Is it a history of the relationship of women to the media as objects of representation, as professionals and workers, as audience members and media producers? Or is it a history of feminist ideas, feminist theory, and feminist research about communication practices, technologies, and representations?

It certainly can be all of those things and more, but as a respondent said in answering my recent call for stories about feminist communication history, "Our history is still before us."[1] We have history to make, both to produce changes for women and to write feminist narratives of communication and the field. Although much has been written in recent decades about gender and communication, about women and media, and about feminist theory and research, far less has been published that carries our work to another level of recollection and synthesis and that integrates the critique of critical race scholars and postcolonial theorists. Even less of this work has been institutionalized and accounted for by nonfeminist traditions and perspectives. As a result, feminist work in and on communication, as well as the history of feminist work, remains incomplete, marginalized, or even altogether absent in how the field accounts for the ideas, people, research, and concerns of those who constitute the field and what we study. Instead, "Monopolies of Knowledge"[2] perpetuate a framework of categories of inquiry (most notably discrete areas of interpersonal, rhetorical, organizational, political, and media or mass communication); canonize events, research traditions, and scholars; and frame epistemological and ideological differences. The question of what feminist history is must be preceded with questions about why there is so little feminist history in the field of communication.

These absences, deficiencies, and constraints cannot all be accounted for here, but the groundwork might be laid for some of the work ahead for feminist scholars and nonfeminist scholars alike. This chapter, then, is not an attempt to write a feminist history of communication or of media studies, which is needed, but it will attempt to lay out components of a feminist historiography for our field: a study of the methods, practices, results, and possibilities of writing our histories. It will explore the practice of making history in communication, the problems of history in communication, and the state and development of feminist history in communication. The experiences and ideas of twenty-five feminist colleagues who responded to a call to participate in making feminist communication history have contributed to the themes. Their ideas and stories were solicited through a call made on e-mail and through the listservs of six associations and organizational divisions important to feminist scholars in communication. Respondents provided answers to a set of initial questions, then were given an opportunity to review a draft of this chapter and make suggestions and corrections. Their insights were invaluable, but any shortcomings in the argument are my own. The exercise in collecting feminists' histories made it clear, as I explain later, that the work of writing our histories, like all history-making, is complex and contestable. As one respondent concluded, "What you seek to account for may be more elusive than it seems."

A FEMINIST CHALLENGE TO MEDIA HISTORIOGRAPHY

Like any other academic discipline whose history is called into question by feminist thinking,[3] our work must continue to critique the historical practices, or practices of making history, that predominate in our field. Despite excellent historical work by some feminist communication scholars, the foundational work of feminist historians on historiography such as Linda Kerber, Gerda Lerner, Sheila Rowbotham, Joan Wallach Scott, and Bonnie G. Smith has made little headway into our field.[4] Feminist historians help us see the deficiency of history-making (telling narratives about history) that hides gender at the same time that gender systems and gendered meanings serve a fundamental organizing role in most societies; the deficiency of history-making that valorizes history made "from the top" and history made by "great men"; the deficiency of history-making that assumes a grand narrative of a progressive and linear development of events, epics, and consequences; and the deficiency of history-making that reifies structures of power and domination through an acceptance and valuation of the public over the private, the expert over the amateur, the episodic over the everyday. Further, their work points out that professional history-making as an academic practice has its own gendered trajectory wrapped in changing definitions of masculinity and femininity.[5]

Such history-making and its discontents remain the norm rather than the exception in the field of media research history, in which "great men, great events, great places" have been used to make a historical canon repeated in introductory undergraduate textbooks and graduate textbooks on communication theory and research. Critical scholars have also challenged the discursive primacy of "mass communication research,"[6] but too often substitute their own list of "great men, great events, and great places," without a radical reconsideration of approach. David Berry and John Theobald's *Radical Mass Media Criticism* uses the same approach but substituting names, places, and publication events of critical male scholars, with the sole exception of Cynthia Carter's chapter on bell hooks.[7] John Durham Peters and Peter Simonson's collection, *Mass Communication and American Social Thought: Key Texts, 1920–1968*, follows a similar pattern, key men and key texts, with few exceptions.[8]

Great Men

Students of the dominant mass communication research paradigm would have no trouble reciting any number of "fathers" of American communication research, a list that might include Harold Lasswell, Paul Lazarsfeld, and Walter Lippmann, while critical and cultural scholars might name John Dewey, Stuart Hall, Theodor Adorno, and Michel Foucault. An example of how the "great man" theme has been reified in the field even if the names are changed is revealed by James Beniger's project to identify the 120 "most important" theorists of communication based on the number of mentions in the *International Encyclopedia of Communications*.[9] He singled out 120 individuals representing several disciplines with birth dates ranging chronologically from 469 B.C. (Socrates) to 1941, from entries by a group of 465 "distinguished" authorities from a preponderance of "elite institutions." Only two of the "most important" theorists are women, Margaret Mead and Julia Kristeva. Beniger dismisses Bernard Berelson's claim of four "Founding Fathers" of the field (Kurt Lewin, Paul Lazarsfeld, Harold Lasswell, and Carl Hovland) in favor of this new group, which Beniger heralds as the newly recognized intellectual core of the field. Beniger has made a step forward by opening up the intellectual genealogy of the field to reflection and inspection and embracing the influence of ideas from outside the discipline, but he falls prey to the same logic that feminist communication scholars have exposed in refuting the authority of reference works such as dictionaries and encyclopedias.[10] Because women, and certainly feminists, have historically been discredited as authorities, and have been seriously underrepresented at "prestigious" institutions, the encyclopedia and Beniger's list reaffirms the patrilineage of the field.

Great Places

The history of mass communication theory and research is often attached to particular groups of people centered at or from a location, with a common approach or research agenda. This practice has been employed by the dominant research tradition as well as its critics. The names often referenced as schools of thought if not institutional location are the Columbia School, the Chicago School, Yale, the Frankfurt School, the Birmingham Centre, and the Toronto School. All but Yale (with the Birmingham Centre replaced by the term British Cultural Studies) are used as an organizing framework for proposing and dissecting canonized texts in media research in a recent book edited by Elihu Katz, John Durham Peters, Tamar Liebes, and Avril Orloff.[11] The extent to which feminism cannot be forced into the categories is revealed by the unintended irony in the last chapter's title (and the only one devoted to feminist work), "Afterthoughts on Mulvey's 'Visual Pleasure' in the Age of Cultural Studies."[12] If feminist journalism historians have struggled to bring women "Up From the Footnotes,"[13] feminist scholars struggle to make feminist theory and history more than an afterthought. Feminist scholarship exists both within and across the grain of these sites of research; consequently, a history of feminist work would account for feminist thinking in each school of thought as well as in its own right.

Great Times

A third common feature of the field's histories are those that follow a chronological theme of events or periods. For almost twenty-five years, Lowery and DeFleur have canonized certain research projects, on media "processes and effects," and impressed them into historical consciousness as "milestones."[14] They included the Payne Fund studies on movies, the invasion from Mars "radio panic," the "people's choice" exercised through voting behavior, persuasion in World War II, personal influence, message diffusion, and the problems of comic books, television, and children. Other standard histories have incorporated the milestones into broader accounts of social change in the United States.[15] The milestone method maps onto an approach to media history that follows the same linear, progressive, and deterministic logic represented in introductory undergraduate textbooks. Media technologies are taken up chronologically, in order of appearance in the United States, in a progressive account of technological invention, economic and technological determinism, and social change. Cultural and critical theorists are more likely to think in longer epics than research events and to take an interest in the greater sweep of cultural change associated with technological, political and economic, and intellectual trends. Even so, thinking of history as great eras of research or communication systems reifies rather than questions dominant trajectories and obscures counter strands of thought and experience.

THE STATE OF FEMINIST HISTORY

Such history-making in the field of communication has not been without its challenges and contributions from feminist scholars, who have engaged with history on specific topics and have constructed some larger narratives that account for our work. The task is formidable: to retell stories of communication, of technology, and of the field that account for women across cultures and contexts, for gender systems, for academic practices, for feminist activism, and for feminist theorizing. Despite the size of the task, feminists have challenged conventional histories, claimed women's communication in its historic context, and begun to construct new eras and problematics that account for feminist theory. We have clearly been less successful engaging with issues of race, culture, class, and nationality, and we must renew our commitment to examine the white- and U.S.-centrism of our work.

Challenging Conventional Histories

To challenge conventional histories, scholars have needed to question the methods of conventional historiography and recover documents and experiences that illuminate alternative perspectives on women's media, women communicators, and women's presence in the field.[16] The problem of historiography in communication has been addressed in various critiques like Sue Curry Jansen's (1993)—a paper still relevant today on the absence of women's experiences and of feminist analysis from historical accounts of communication research.[17] New methods of recovering women's experiences in the field are illustrated by Therese L. Lueck's use of interviews and historical records for her narrative of the history of women educators as activists and scholars working through the Commission on the Status of Women of the Association for Education in Journalism and Mass Communication (AEJMC).[18] Other challenges and contributions to new histories have been written over the past thirty years.[19]

Angharad Valdivia and Sarah Projansky have recently provided an extensive summary of feminist media research in its historical context, reviewing bodies of work on texts, production, and audiences as well as on specific media.[20] Karen

Foss, Sonja Foss, and Cindy Griffin sorted their review of feminist work, most of it outside of journalism and mass communication, into a systematic challenge to the field's history of theory and research.[21] They observe that events, projects, journals, conferences, and associations have been pivotal to the direction of feminist agendas, and they develop a taxonomy of the development of feminist perspectives:

> (1) radical beginnings; (2) efforts to include women as communicators and women's topics in the discipline; (3) critiques of the discipline from feminist perspectives; (4) labeling and refining of feminist perspectives; and (5) reconceptualizations of constructs and theories in rhetorical studies from feminist perspectives.[22]

Their taxonomy, similar to stages of curriculum transformation used by feminist and critical race scholars in the past decades, is useful for identifying work being done and the work ahead.

Claiming Women's Communication

Recovering women's means of communicating (including histories of women's media, histories of women journalists and writers, the role of technologies in women's lives and in the construction of gender, and analysis of women's talk and gendered discourse) is critical and far from complete.[23] Some work now challenges the received view of women in the dominant empirical research tradition, such as Susan Douglas's examination of the canonical *Personal Influence*,[24] a good beginning. Histories of women and feminist publications enable us to challenge even critical historical accounts, as Maria Dicenzo has done recently.[25] Despite these revisions and reframings in specific subspecialty areas, comprehensive reconceptualizing of the field and its subject matter remains to be done and integrated with histories of race, culture, and nationality. White feminists, including myself, would benefit from reviewing the foundations for that work, such as found in Angharad Valdivia's argument for multicultural feminist media studies, Jane Rhodes's analysis of voice and definitions of race, Rahda Hegde's assessment of transnational and postcolonial feminism, and Lisa Flores's exploration of perspectives on gender and race in intercultural contexts.[26]

THE CHALLENGES OF MAKING FEMINIST HISTORY

Much of our historical work lies before us, then. To contribute to the effort to imagine and expand the history of feminist communication scholarship, to trace intellectual genealogies, scholarly networks, and opinions about key moments and trends, I sought out the memories and stories of other feminist scholars in creating new accounts of our past and in illuminating the characteristics of a feminist historiography. Contrary to Beniger's appreciation of the work of certain authorities at elite institutions, feminist history, in keeping with feminist epistemology and research generally, should be broadly inclusive, incorporating a wide range of experiences and perspectives. In addition, our experiences are an important source of knowledge, as Gertrude J. Robinson has noted:

> [T]he role of lived experience which previously lacked credence as a source of knowledge, can now be accessed for theory building. Together these liberating practices enable us to include ourselves and our experiences in explaining *why* and *how* we do our intellectual work.[27]

Similarly, Linda Steiner has made the case that autobiographies are useful and important textual artifacts that provide "a way of understanding cultural politics and 'author-ity'" and reveal responses to workplace changes and professional interactions.[28]

This chapter's project became an exercise in the challenges of writing feminist history as well as of the practice of women's communication. A call for contributions was made through six associations of importance to feminist scholarship in communication: the Commission on the Status of Women (CSW) of the AEJMC; the Feminist Scholarship Division (FSD) of the International Communication Association (ICA); the Organization for Research on Women and Communication (ORWAC); the Organization for the Study of Communication, Language, and Gender (OSCLG); the Feminist and Women Studies Division of the National Communication Association (NCA); and the Gender and Communication Section of the International Association of Media and Communication Research (IAMCR).[29] The timing of the call (over the December 2006 holidays) and the quick turnaround required for responses (to keep on deadline for the editors and publisher) limited responses. Twenty-five feminist scholars responded, most with considerable enthusiasm.[30] Responses came mostly from the United States but with some representation from other countries, and included well-established feminist scholars as well as some who questioned whether they would be considered feminist scholars, some with a long history in the field and some with very little. Because of the small number, the project should be classified as an experiment or beginning in gathering histories rather than a finished accomplishment. A larger project in which responses are encouraged over an extended period, representing a range of racial, ethnic, and global perspectives, may be a task for these associations to take up collaboratively.

Feminist scholars were asked to respond electronically to six questions: Which authors and literature were informative and formative in your development as a feminist communication scholar? What are your significant recollections of your earliest participation in scholarly communication associations as a feminist scholar? (Which associations, when?) Who were the feminist "forerunners" in our field who inspired, motivated, taught, or served as a model for you? What and when do you think were the key trends, strands, disappointments, and/or turning points in feminist scholarship in communication? What is your assessment of the field's account of and for feminist scholarship? Anything else about the history of feminist scholarship in communication we should remember?

CONTRIBUTIONS TO FEMINIST COMMUNICATION HISTORY

What were the responses?

Answers to questions one and three, identifying authors, literature, and forerunners, were not clearly distinguishable from each other. There was considerable overlap between authors inside and outside the field who were considered to have both provided ideas that sparked and illuminated their thinking and who inspired and motivated them (either through their personal and professional relationships with the respondent or their public visibility and activism). I had hoped that asking a question about "forerunners" might uncover recollections of individuals before the 1970s, an era in need of attention, but none were identified. Instead, those mentioned were mostly "co-runners," as someone dubbed them, an apt name for the growing group of feminists who advocated, supported, and produced feminist work in the 1970s and beyond.

Despite a number of repetitions, respondents identified 190 different individuals (all women except three) and an organization (the American Association of University Women) that influenced them through their writings or support or both. The names fall into two categories. The first group is made up of women (and two men) in the academic field of communication. They authored works that respondents believed made a significant difference in how they viewed the status of women (in the field or in communication professions), understood gender, and approached the study of communication. Many of the authors of these works were also noted as influential, along with other individuals who might or might not be feminist but who were considered strong and encouraging women. These women were considered significant to respondents' feeling included and supported at conferences, having models for taking political action in the associations, and advocating the need for feminist perspectives on and in communication. In all, 106 individuals in the academic discipline were mentioned.[31]

Women (and one man prominent in masculinity studies) outside of the academic discipline of communication comprised a second group significant to the thinking and research of respondents. These are theorists from other disciplines as well as public scholars and figures. Included in this group of eighty-four individuals (see Table 4.1) are feminist philosophers, feminist theologians, feminist sociologists, women's rights advocates, and feminist activists from the nineteenth century through the twentieth century, and women journalists and other writers. Those identified ranged from Betty Friedan (*Feminine Mystique*), Carol Gilligan (*In a Different Voice*), bell hooks (*From Margin to Center*), Luce Irigaray (*This Sex Which is Not One*), Thersesa de Lauretis (*Technologies of Gender*), Patricia Hill Collins (*Black Feminist Thought*), Rosa Luxemburg (*Social Reform or Revolution*), Batya Weinbaum (*Pictures of Patriarchy*), and Fatima Mernissi (*Women's Rebellion and Islamic Memory*). Clearly, both lists are not exhaustive: other feminist communication scholars will have names to add. As a step toward constructing a genealogy (matrilineal rather than patrilineal) of ideas relevant to feminist work in communication, a table of individuals outside of the discipline of communication is included (see Table 4.1). It is one small corrective step to Beniger's list of top theorists.

Table 4.1. A sampling of contributors to the history of ideas in communication

Individual authors and public figures outside of the academic field of communication identified by a group of scholars as significant to their development as feminist communication scholars.

Abzug, Bella
Acker, Joan
Alexander, Shana
Anthony, Susan B.
Anzaldua, Gloria
Atwood, Margaret
Barrett, Michelle
Bartky, Sandra Lee
Benderly, Beryl
Benedict, Helen
Bosmajian, Hamida
Butler, Judith
Christ, Carol
Cixous, Helene
Cockburn, Cynthia
Collins, Patricia Hill
Daly, Mary

De Beauvoir, Simone
de Lauretis, Theresa
Dickinson, Emily
Donovan, Josephine
Duniway, Abigail Scott
Dworkin, Andrea
Eisenstein, Zillah
Eiserly, Riane
Elgin, Suzette Baden
Enlow, Cynthia
Faludi, Susan
Flax, Jane
Ferguson, Kathy
Fraser, Nancy
Friedan, Betty
Gherardi, Silvia
Gilligan, Carol
Gilman, Charlotte Perkins
Goldman, Emma
Gottfried, Heidi
Haraway, Donna
Harding, Sandra
hooks, bell
Irigaray, Luce
Johnson, Sonja
Kanter, Rosabeth Moss
Kimmel, Michael
King, Carole
Kristeva, Julia
Le Guin, Ursula
Lorde, Audre
Luxemburg, Rosa
Mani, Lata
MacKinnon, Catherine
Mernissi, Fatima
Montenegro, Sofia
Morgan, Robin
Morton, Nelle
Mulvey, Laura
Parsons, Elsie Clews
Piercy, Marge
Plath, Sylvia
Rich, Adrienne
Richardson, Laurel
Ruether, Rosemary Radford
Sandler, Berenice
Sarton, May

Scott, Joan
Simon, Carly
Spivak, Gayatri
Stanton, Elizabeth Cady
Starhawk
Steinem, Gloria
Taylor, Verta
Tong, Rosemary
Vance, Carole
Walker, Alice
Weedon, Chris
Weinbaum, Batya
Welty, Eudora
Willard, Frances
Williams, Judith
Wilson-Kastner, Patricia
Wollstonecraft, Mary
Woodhull, Victoria
Woolf, Virginia
Zita, Jacquelyn

Respondents emphasized how the works they read provided intellectual, professional, and personal turning points for them. One respondent said:

> In 1982, when I was a student in a major university's master of science in journalism program, I somehow came across a copy of *Women in Media: A Documentary Source Book*, edited by Maurine Beasley and Sheila Gibbons . . . I don't remember where I got it, but I remember carrying it around like a Bible. With its short historical biographies of women journalists and its radical "Principles of Feminist Journalism" it was somehow a sacred text to me—in part because it was in every way different from my journalism program, where all the professors were male except one and where I was afraid to take one of the required classes because I'd heard that the professor had taken off his shoe and thrown it across the room at a female student. The truth was, I hated the program. Journalism felt shallow and false to me . . . In some way I couldn't articulate at the time, the book felt true to me. The problem was, I didn't know what to do with it.

Work from other disciplines was equally influential. Feminist work may not have been included in respondents' undergraduate or graduate programs, requiring them to find it on their own or rely on advice from role models in other disciplines on their campuses. One respondent said:

> But in the 1980s when I was coming through graduate studies, I read widely in several fields and this really helped me situate feminist communication scholarship in the larger developing landscape of feminist scholarship.

Other respondents noted that what they read led them to important discoveries that gender is a social construction or a performance, that intersections of race, class, gender, and sexuality are critical but difficult and complex, and that cultural, global, and religious contexts must be accounted for.

Second, respondents identified particular moments that spurred their identification with feminist issues or with feminist scholarship. These are autobiographical moments involving a positive or negative experience with a paper accepted or presented, a panel or speaker attended, a significant moment in an association's history, the exclusion, or invisibility of women in conferences or events, or a relationship with a feminist colleague begun. For example, there were negative experiences:

> There were few bonding moments with other women for me. Everywhere I looked the scholars were men and the professors were men... My dean told me to abandon research about women in media management because I could more easily get tenure with my agenda setting research... I didn't like that either and didn't listen. It angered me that anyone would suggest feminist work wasn't worthy or tenurable ... I realized early on that the communication conventions I attended had rules about scholarship and feminist work was not particularly well-received.

Another woman said:

> The first time I went to AEJMC was in 1979—when the association still had its annual meetings at university campuses. I distinctly recall going into the cafeteria at lunchtime—so this would be the best opportunity to see the "whole" of the membership, as opposed to smaller audiences at individual sessions—and being greeted by a sea of white men in short-sleeved blue shirts, only distinguished, it seemed to me, by whether they had white hair or were bald. Frankly, my first question was why the average age skewed so high—but again, this was at a point when the membership was very dominated by former/retired journalists. The very next thought was, where are the women? At some party I met some women, but nearly all of them were the wives of these men; they took tours during the day during the convention, and then returned at night. And nearly every man I met asked me to whom I was married, assuming that I was hanging around because I was married to an AEJMC member.

Not everyone's experience with an association was negative:

> I joined AEJMC in 1976 and have attended every convention since then (through 2006 except for the year 1977). In the early years I found support from exemplary individuals. . . I participated in the activities of the Commission on the Status of Women and found it a congenial group. I must say I did not find much (if any) hostility from male scholars in AEJMC. Perhaps by the time I was really involved in the organization (the 1980s) the groundwork for women's participation had been laid by others.